A Woman's Struggle

A Woman's Struggle

Alfred J. Fortino

to the Towerseys
In memory of two generations
of acquaintance
Alfred J Fortino

VANTAGE PRESS
New York

This is a work of fiction. Any similarity between
the characters appearing herein and any real persons,
living or dead, is purely coincidental.

Cover design by Susan Thomas

FIRST EDITION

Published by Vantage Press, Inc.
516 West 34th Street, New York, New York 10001

Manufactured in the United States of America
ISBN: 0-533-13662-8

Library of Congress Catalog Card No.: 00-92160

0 9 8 7 6 5 4 3 2 1

Introduction

Through the Internet, information about you is not only readily available but can be instantaneously communicated to the rest of the world. If you are arrested and charged with a crime, you must win in two courts—the court of law and the court of public opinion. You can win in a court of law and be acquitted of guilt but lose in the court of public opinion and suffer lifelong punishment.

The trial in the court of public opinion is much harder on the defendant. You cannot plead the Fifth Amendment and remain silent without prejudice to your cause. There is not even a presumption of innocence. If the media puts a spin on the facts and introduces salacious gossip to make for a more titillating story, there may be a presumption of guilt and a clamor for punishment before the trial even starts.

A woman working in the business world is handicapped. Intelligence and experience are often enough for a man to succeed, but a woman must also be physically attractive. Legislation intended to stop discrimination does not reach into our hearts and minds.

Finally, in a world in which love is sex and sex is love, a love which professes to transcend sex is met with derision.

I thought about these things as I read the Lansing, Michigan *State Journal* and drank my morning coffee.

A Woman's Struggle

1

"LAKE ACQUITTED!" the headlines screamed, the two words filling a quarter of the front page of the *State Journal.* No more was necessary. Everybody in Lansing knew about the only society murder committed in this otherwise peaceful capital of the state of Michigan.

I sipped my coffee, stared at the silent phone, then sighed and read the story:

> Arthur Lake, prominent local businessman was found "not guilty" by a jury of his peers after only two hours of deliberation. Charged with having murdered his handicapped wife with a lethal dose of morphine, Lake, according to Prosecuting Attorney John Traver, wanted to rid himself of his wheelchair-bound wife who suffered from multiple sclerosis. Prosecution witnesses testified that Lake had an on-going affair with his business associate, Martha Smith.
>
> Called to the stand, Martha Smith admitted loving the accused and claimed he loved her. The crime was allegedly committed in Heritage Hospital under the noses of several nurses, but the murder weapon, a vial of morphine, has never been found and, according to Traver, was most likely destroyed by Arthur Lake after he'd used it to kill Hannah.

I took another sip, leaned back in my chair, and went on reading, undisturbed by clients or solicitors.

> A glamorous business executive, Martha Smith is the mother of Hollywood starlet Michelle Morgan. The sometime companion

of Jimmy Smith, aging matinee idol and former NFL halfback, Michelle did not appear at the trial and when contacted refused to comment on her mother's involvement with accused murderer Arthur Lake, bolstering suspicion among celebrity-watchers of an estrangement between mother and daughter.

Arthur Lake did not testify on his own behalf, leaving many Lansing residents wondering what he had to hide.

I had followed the story of the trial in the news because the starlet Michelle Morgan was Michelle Smith, a classmate of mine in Eastern High School in Lansing. She was the most beautiful girl I had ever known. From a distance I had admired her for her personality as well as her beauty. I had fantasized about dating her. However, she was a member of the very rich family of Martha Smith and I was a poor boy from the wrong side of the tracks. I knew that if I should ask her for a date I would be politely turned down. Martha Smith I had known only by her reputation. She, too, was a beauty but she was also known as a very tough business woman who had made a lot of money. When I was in high school she was active in real estate, selling and developing. Now she was a rich landlord. I had no interest in her. I was a secret admirer of her daughter. It was no surprise to me that Michelle had become a movie star. She had been active in drama in high school. She had gone from high school to Stanford University so she could be near Hollywood. Her twin sister, Melinda, was known as "the brain." But Michelle was one of those girls who was more than attractive. She was bewitching.

As a young lawyer, only two years out of law school, the case intrigued me not only because of my acquaintance with Michelle but because it was an interesting murder mystery. My own practice was limited to drawing up deeds, contracts, and wills, with now and then a divorce case for excitement. I operated out of a tiny two-room office in a downtown two-story building and had a part-time secretary on call. I had no real vices, unless staying up late to watch old movies could be considered a vice. I was single, lived frugally, and had plenty of time to follow the case in the newspaper and to pretend I was the chief prosecutor or defense attorney. I could have argued the case either way, but like most people, I was surprised by the "not guilty" verdict. The letters to the editor of the *Journal* almost unanimously condemned the jury's decision.

Martha Smith had practically admitted under oath that she and the defendant were lovers, but in his summation Defense Attorney Tim Moynihan claimed Hannah Lake was afflicted with multiple sclerosis and was in great pain. She asked to receive no further treatment and be allowed to die. Any one of the nurses could have administered the lethal dose of morphine on the pretext of alleviating the pain. Dr. Archer testified that it was an extra twenty milligrams of morphine which had caused death. Apparently the jury was not convinced beyond a reasonable doubt that the patient had been poisoned. Moreover, no one had seen Lake administer the extra dose.

I was driven by a solid hunch that there was much more to the case than had appeared in print—and by deeply submerged hope that I might at least become acquainted with the girl of my dreams. Of course it also occurred to me that if I could come up with some startling evidence to positively prove Lake's guilt or innocence I might make a good name for myself. Maybe I could move out of my shabby office into the new high-rise office building close to the courthouse.

Once socially prominent, Arthur Lake and Martha Smith were now social outcasts. Rumors in barbershops, beauty salons, coffee shops, and backyards had it that the two had colluded to kill Hannah Lake. They became pariahs in the business world as potential clients shunned them and fellow realtors stopped doing business with them. The media hounded them incessantly. Television cameras were at their respective homes and paparazzi vied with one another to get pictures of the couple engaging in intimacy, or, failing that, holding hands. Anytime they were together at any gathering, newspaper reporters and television cameras focused on them.

Celebrities deal with invasion of their privacy in ingenious ways, but Lake and Smith were thrust unprepared into the limelight. Celebrities are worshipped; Lake and Smith suffered public disdain and condemnation. *This is what OJ Simpson has had to endure,* I thought, tossing the paper on the desk. The front page photos of Arthur Lake and Martha Smith seemed to glower at me, and I thought, *But what if someone condemned by public opinion was in fact innocent? What if Lake and Smith were innocent? How would they reclaim their lives?*

These startling and disturbing thoughts had never occurred to me before. Perhaps my interest in Michelle led me to such thought. If I was going to investigate this case, it would have to be in terms the public could accept. The rules of law were not the same as those governing public opinion, and I would have to proceed very carefully.

To prove Lake and Smith guilty or innocent and convince the public my evidence had to be unassailable, I would need media contacts and sales techniques, both of which would help me in my career. I had no wife or family to support, no debts, and my overhead for rent and utilities expenses was minimal. As I turned on the answering machine and locked the office, my mind raced ahead. I could write articles for the *Bar Journal* to recover expenditures. Obviously I could not know that in embarking on this venture I was changing my life.

Intrigued as I was, I climbed into my five-year-old Mercury Sable and drove across town to visit John Traver, whom I knew well enough to address by his first name. Old enough to be my father, John was in his middle forties, of average height, and with a full head of hair graying at the temples. He was a good lawyer and I had learned a lot watching him question witnesses, but he was in a foul mood when I met him in the prosecutor's office in the courthouse.

My first question clearly annoyed him. "Did Arthur Lake intentionally kill his wife, or did he only want to lessen her pain and negligently gave her too much morphine?"

"What difference does it make what I think?" he demanded. "The jury has spoken." Under his breath he muttered, "The jury is an ass."

"Why was Murder One the only charge brought?" I persisted. "The jury might have convicted Lake of a lesser charge, manslaughter or negligent homicide."

He shook his head. "Everybody in this office thought negligent homicide was the proper charge, a case about a man who tried to alleviate his wife's pain and did what he knew he should not do, knowing full well that morphine might kill her. I didn't think we could get a conviction on that charge. A jury was not likely to put a man in prison when he had no intent to kill his wife, simply wanted to ease her pain. I brought a charge of murder because I was satisfied that this guy was in love with a beautiful younger woman. He figured out a neat way of getting rid of his wife. Any way you look at it, that's murder, and I was sure a jury would convict. Of course, we had no eye witnesses."

"Why would he kill her when she was already on her death bed?" I asked.

He shrugged. "Maybe he couldn't wait. Maybe his so-called 'partner' was pressuring him, dangling it in front of him, so to speak. She testified that they had not been lovers, though they were in love. I don't believe it; it flies in the face of reason and human nature. But if it's true maybe Lake couldn't wait to get his hands on her. Multiple sclerosis can go into remission; Lake knew that because his wife had had remissions, and Dr. Morgan Archer, who was in charge of the case, told him it was possible. Remission was exactly what Lake wanted to avoid.

That's why he gave her a lethal dose of morphine. It's as clear as the nose on your face, but the jury wouldn't buy it."

I touched my nose. It was sunburned and peeling, and I was self-conscious about it. Aside from my nose, and my ears which turned bright red whenever I was embarrassed, I wasn't bad looking, or so I'd been told. I was six feet tall and had a good physique. People were always trying to fix me up with their cousin or niece, an impulse that almost always ended disastrously. Good looking or not, I was no ladies' man. For my age, I was a good trial lawyer and could think on my feet, but on a date with a stranger I was awkward as a teenager, blushed fiercely, and usually said the wrong thing. I asked good questions and could create a mental picture of a scene from scattered comments, but a pretty girl could tie my tongue in knots with a suggestive smile. Perhaps that's another reason I had not dared approach Michelle.

Traver fixed his eyes on me. "What say you, Mark Pierce, Esquire? Guilty or no?"

"I don't know. I didn't hear the testimony, and I don't trust newspapers' anonymous rewrite editors. Harriet Owens covered the trial for the *Journal*, didn't she?" Traver nodded. "She seems to have as much journalistic integrity as anyone. Do you know her?"

"Ask a lawyer a straightforward question and watch him dance." The prosecutor shuffled his feet. "Feint, dodge, and sidestep for the defense. I thought you were different, Pierce, a breed apart, honest to a fault. I may have misjudged you."

"Because I won't say Lake killed his wife? How could you be so sure he did it when you had no eyewitness?"

"Murderers don't usually kill people in front of eyewitnesses. What we had were facts which were never disputed." Traver raised a finger. "The victim was receiving ten milligrams of morphine over a period of four hours." He raised a second finger. "The residue of free morphine in the urine after death is always ten percent of the dose administered." Up went a third finger. "The residue should have been one milligram if the patient got only ten milligrams, but there were *three* milligrams of free morphine in the urine of the deceased." He looked at his hand; it shook slightly. He made a fist. "Therefore, the patient got an extra twenty milligrams. At the same time a twenty milligram vial of morphine turned up missing at a time when the only person at the nurse's station where the morphine was kept was Arthur Lake. Twenty milligrams of morphine on top of ten, a lethal dose, particularly when introduced in a matter of minutes."

"Who trained Lake to inject a twenty-milligram vial of morphine into his wife's bloodstream in a matter of minutes?" I asked. "I wouldn't know how to do that."

Traver smiled avuncularly. "If you were an ambulance chaser who hung around the emergency room, you'd pick it up in no time, a bright fellow like you. In Mrs. Lake's case, it was necessary to administer antibiotics quite often. She was prone to urinary infections, you see. The plastic tube which carried the morphine had an enlarged aperture through which antibiotics could be introduced, quickly and in large doses. It was a simple matter for Lake to get the morphine from the closet where he knew it was stored and dump it into the antibiotic aperture. Of course nobody saw him do this."

"And you never found the empty morphine vial."

"No. If he had tossed it into a trash bin it would have been retrieved. All trash is screened for drugs to prevent stealing.

"But isn't morphine always kept in a locked closet?"

"Yes," Traver replied. "And the key was in the possession of the charge nurse who admitted that on that hot, late May day she had removed her white coat containing the key and hung it in her locker at the nurse's station. Lake made his move when the nurses responded to an emergency. He slipped the key from the charge nurse's locker, unlocked the closet, and put the key back before anyone noticed it missing. Mrs. Lake's room was next to the station, so he had ample time to do this. The nurses were gone for several minutes."

"If no one noticed that the key was missing, isn't that mere conjecture?"

Traver smiled. "The key was not missing. Lake put it back in the nurse's pocket before the nurse returned. It was a week later when the morphine was needed that the vial was missed."

"And that was your case?" I queried.

"No. There were two other important facts. Lake had asked Doctor Archer to provide more morphine for his wife. He claimed he had her power of attorney and that she preferred death to excruciating pain. Archer of course refused. There was also his affair with Martha Smith, a younger, very attractive woman."

"When was the body discovered?"

"When the nurses got back to their station one of them looked into Mrs. Lake's room. She appeared to be asleep, and he was simply sitting there. The nurse made no further inquiry. It was almost an hour before Lake went home. About an hour later, when the nurse went to check on the patient, she found Mrs. Lake dead."

"How do you know twenty milligrams of morphine were used on Mrs. Lake?"

"The hospital is required to keep records of all narcotics and how they are administered. There was no record that any of the twenty milligrams were used on anyone."

I checked my watch; it was almost three in the afternoon. "Can I buy you lunch?" I asked and was relieved when Traver shook his head. He must have been even more relieved to see me go.

2

I left the DA's office with more questions than answers. Having convinced himself of Arthur Lake's guilt, John Traver couldn't understand why the jury had failed to accept his conclusion. I wondered how the defense saw Lake, so I made an appointment to see Tim Moynihan, arrived fifteen minutes ahead of time, and parked at a meter around the corner from the attorney's well-appointed office. Moynihan was a tall, bald man in his fifties who impressed me with his modest demeanor. Moynihan didn't go in for flashy clothes like some defense lawyers. He was quiet, self-controlled and had a subtle, dry sense of humor. He was considered one of the best defense lawyers in the state, which was no doubt why Lake had chosen him. He was a sole practitioner with offices in a single two-story office complex across from the capital, much like mine but almost luxurious.

I expected he was pleased with the verdict and did not insult him by asking if he was surprised, for he would respond that the verdict was precisely what he had expected. Instead, I asked if he was surprised by the public outrage following Lake's acquittal.

"Not at all," Moynihan replied, showing me to a chair. "He has three strikes against him: he's rich, he's got an attractive business partner, and he's innocent. How could anyone like a guy like that?"

I didn't know if he was serious, and Moynihan laughed at my confusion. Blushing, I stammered, "He—Lake—can't be tried again; that would be double jeopardy; so, just tell me if he administered morphine to his wife."

Moynihan relaxed into a massive leather chair behind a highly polished, bare desk and said, "He has not answered that question and I won't answer it either. As you said, my client is being tried in the court of public opinion. He is being tried daily by people who will continue to dismiss the Fifth Amendment and other Constitutional rights until the day they are unjustly accused themselves. To them, the Fifth Amendment is something for criminals to hide behind. In fact, they've already convicted Lake, and sentenced him to public exile. Not only is he ostracized, so too is Martha Smith, and she's never been charged with anything."

"But if they're innocent and I can persuade the public that they're innocent, won't they be exonerated in the court of public opinion?"

Moynihan thought about it for a moment, then said, "I don't believe it to be in my client's interest for you to delve into this story all over again."

I felt he was hiding something. I pressed him to be more forthcoming. "Tell me why it's not in your client's interest for the public to hear from you that Arthur Lake did not intend to kill his wife and that he did not overdose her with morphine."

Moynihan smiled. "Suppose I told you that Arthur Lake never administered morphine to his wife, never intended to end her life. What would be the result of that? Would it stop the horrible stories? The public wouldn't believe it for a minute. They don't want to believe it. Rather, they would think we were part of the cover-up. They would censure us as surely as they have censured Arthur and Martha."

"You're thinking of your reputation, not theirs," I muttered.

"How pleasant it must be not to have to worry about yours," he said affably. Then, before I could respond, he said, "And suppose that Mr. Lake were to say to you, 'Yes, I killed my wife'? That would make a farce of the Fifth Amendment.

The public would then be justified in believing that taking the Fifth is just an escape route for guilty people. We don't dare insult the American legal system that way. No, we choose to assert our Fifth Amendment rights even in the court of public opinion. It is not a court indictment we fear, it is a public indictment."

"I'm interested in this case precisely because of the dilemma you have just described. I want to answer the very same questions the public is asking. We're not dealing with a larceny gone awry or some other venal prelude to murder. The public is upset because there's more here than meets the eye."

"Mencken said 'The public is an ass,' and I tend to agree with that son of Baltimore."

"With all due respect," I said, "I have a higher regard for Americans than that."

Moynihan leaned back in his chair. "Well, you're young yet. It would be sad if you weren't idealistic. Unfortunately, there's no way we can overcome the intriguing stories and speculations indulged in by the media. Would you favor passing a law that once a verdict were entered it would be a crime for anyone to challenge it?"

"Of course not."

"Neither would I," Moynihan said, rising to indicate the interview was over.

We shook hands and parted affably, but as I descended the marble stairs to the tastefully furnished lobby I began to question my ability to pierce the polished if contradictory accounts presented by the prosecution and defense. I'd been stonewalled by professionals, and I didn't know why they felt it necessary to do so, but if I was sure of anything it was that Traver and Moynihan were both withholding information vital to understanding what had really happened to Hannah Lake.

I tried to follow Moynihan's reasoning. His clients (assuming he also represented Martha Smith, and I almost turned back to pose the question then kicked myself for not having done so earlier) were suffering. Lake and Smith were holed up in their respective houses with television cameras pointed at their front doors, yet Moynihan had reason to let them suffer. Suppose Arthur Lake were to say, "I did not overdose my wife with morphine," the next question would be "Where were you at the time of the alleged overdosing?" Witnesses had testified he was at the scene of the crime. He was there before the nurses left to attend to an emergency, and he was there when they came back minutes later. An hour later, Hannah Lake was dead. If someone else had administered the morphine overdose, Arthur would have seen it. Who else would do such a thing and how? *Where was Martha Smith at the time,* I wondered, thunderstruck. Had she been asked when she testified?

Instead of retracing my steps to Moynihan's office, I decided to drive across town to the *Journal* Building. If anyone could help me penetrate the mystery surrounding Hannah Lake's death, Harriet Owens could. "Darn!" I expostulated as I turned the corner and saw a meter maid slipping a parking ticket beneath the wiper blade of my Sable.

"I thought that was your car, counselor," said the meter maid, a pretty young lady named Roxanne Weber who had been a sophomore at Eastern High School when I was a junior, "but I've never heard you use such strong language."

Blushing, I stammered, "S-sorry, excuse me," and got into my car. Driving off, I pounded the steering wheel. "Why did I apologize to her?" I asked myself. "She should have apologized to me for writing that ticket. The meter must have just expired!"

Later that night while brushing my teeth I had realized that Roxanne Weber had also been making fun of me. When I was a senior the Eastern Yearbook had listed me as "Most Courteous," noting that "Gosh is the strangest word in Mark Pierce's vocabulary." It had provoked half the seniors and almost everyone in the lower grades to taunt me, and had I not left for college my face would have stayed red all summer long.

3

There was more to this case than simple murder, but what was it? Harriet Owens wasn't in when I called, but I was able to access the newspaper archives and searched the database for material on Martha Smith and Arthur Lake. Armed with reels of microfilm, I made my way to the library and found an unoccupied film reader and scrolled through magazine articles extolling the virtues of a dynamic woman who had accumulated a fortune of forty to fifty million dollars in a little over twenty years. Martha Smith was co-owner of the Enterprise Building in Lansing. The offices of Lake Realty Co. and Enterprise Properties were located on the fourth floor of the building—the top floor—with the lower floors rented to stock brokers and accountants, a mortgage company, and a title company.

Enterprise Properties owned several small shopping centers located through the Midwest and the South. Martha was on a bank board, on the board of the local Salvation Army, the United Way, and a couple of statewide non-profits. She was an officer on the board of the local chamber of commerce as well. I wondered how long it would take for these organizations to find pretext for dumping her.

Several articles extolled her beauty. She had been nominated female executive of the year, a nomination which was sure to be withdrawn. A fashion magazine featured her as one of the ten best-dressed women of the previous year.

As for Arthur Lake, cursory articles reported on events in which he had participated, meetings of the local realtors' association, community fund drives for Christmas baskets for the poor, and so on. One piece noted he was the husband of Hannah Lake, a disabled woman who suffered from multiple sclerosis but was active in the University Women's Association, the citizens advisory committee to the local school board, and a member of the city library board.

Martha had it all over Arthur when it came to media attention. The stories were not always flattering. One article referred to her as a "dragon lady," a beautiful woman who always got what she wanted. She was accused of using her looks to charm people into signing agreements which earned her big commissions but which were not always to her clients' advantage. An unidentified source said she was a ruthless operator whose influence extended into the state legislature.

The stories confirmed that Martha Smith was in her early forties and the mother of beautiful twin girls, one of whom was movie starlet Michelle Morgan, the other Melinda Trudeau, a doctoral candidate at Duke University engaged in research with her husband Claude, an archeologist. Martha was divorced from a James T. Smith whose whereabouts were unknown.

I was startled by a woman's throaty voice. "Are you finding anything of interest?" I looked up from the microfilm reader to see a tall, handsome woman with flaming, shoulder-length red hair.

"You must be Harriet Owens," I said rising and extending my hand.

"My reputation precedes me," she said, taking my hand in a grip that was almost too firm.

"N-no," I stammered, "I haven't heard anything about you."

"Too bad. What would you like to know?" She hitched up her skirt and sat down at the edge of the table, exposing her thigh. Several years older than me, she dressed like a teenager. Or a streetwalker.

"I'd like to know if you'll have dinner with me this evening," I said, then reddened, surprised by my own audacity. "I beg your . . . I'm sor . . . I don't know what got into me," I said, fumbling for words.

She laughed. "Happens all the time. But I don't think you can afford me."

Had she taken my invitation for a proposition? My ears flamed. "No, I didn't mean—."

"Perfectly all right," she said, patted my cheek as if I were a child, and left the library, swinging her hips. She turned at the door and said, "I'm finishing up a piece on Martha Smith for *Exposé.* Would you like to see it?"

"What will it cost me?" I asked coldly. The only thing I hate more than rejection is condescension.

The svelte reporter for the *Exposé* didn't notice or didn't take it personally. "A couple of shots of Jack Daniels, neat," she said. "Five-thirty tomorrow at the Tap Club. And lose the tie."

"What's wrong with—" but she was gone. I decided to call it quits as well. Two women had infuriated me; that was enough for one day.

Before going home, I stopped at my office to check phone messages. The court reporter had called to inform me that *Exposé* magazine had ordered the trial transcript and I could buy a copy for a third of the price he had previously quoted. "Yes!" I pumped my fist, "something good this way comes!" I raced back across town, caught the court reporter as he was leaving his office, accompanied him to the copy shop and, while 1875 pages were being copied, ordered take-out Hunan chicken and an appetizer from Lee's Chinese.

Meeser, my Siamese cat, yowled at me as I entered, then curled about my leg when he smelled the food. I dumped rice, chicken, and pot stickers into one bowl, doused it all with soy sauce, gave Meeser what was left in the cartons, found a pair of chopsticks that almost matched, and started eating and reading at the kitchen table.

The transcript answered some of my questions. There was a superficial chemical analysis as well as the names of some people I might want to interview. Among these were Smith's and Lake's secretaries, Dr. Morgan Archer, Delores Winfield, and another nurse at Heritage Hospital. There were also the names of witnesses who believed Smith and Lake were man and wife. I was sure that if I could locate these people, I'd be able to find others who could tell me more.

The transcript provided another serious bit of information. Dr. Archer, the complainant in the criminal proceeding, was also the expert witness for the prosecution. I read avidly that portion of the transcript containing his testimony. He claimed that the three milligrams of free morphine found in the urine of the deceased proved that Mrs. Lake had been administered thirty milligrams of morphine, twenty milligrams more than she should have received by his order. He also testified that twenty milligrams administered at once was sufficient to cause cardiac arrest. He based this on the medical standard that the residue in the urine was always 10 percent of what had been administered. He concluded that the deceased received a total of thirty milligrams, twenty milligrams more than had been prescribed, which was the amount of morphine in the missing vial.

On cross-examination, Moynihan showed the death certificate to Dr. Archer and asked, "What is shown as the cause of death?"

Dr. Archer read the certificate and replied, "Multiple sclerosis."

Moynihan then showed the witness the autopsy report. "What is shown as the cause of death on the autopsy?"

"Multiple sclerosis." Archer was shown a third document and asked to identify it. Archer said, "This is the document I put in the file after we discovered that a twenty-milligram vial of morphine was missing."

"How did you know that the urine had three times as much free morphine than should have been there?" Moynihan asked.

"That appears in the autopsy report," Dr. Archer answered.

"When was the missing vial of morphine reported?"

"Some time later."

"A week after the autopsy, wasn't it?"

"That could be; I don't know precisely how long."

"And your report was filed after the vial of morphine was reported missing, right?"

"Yes, sir."

"So, you knew of the excess morphine as soon as you saw the autopsy. When was that completed and shown to you?"

"It was completed twenty-four hours after death."

"Then, why didn't you object to the death certificate and the autopsy immediately and insist then that morphine be shown as the cause of death?"

Archer seemed to answer without hesitation. "The autopsy had shown extensive damage to the myelin in the spinal cord. Without knowledge of the additional dosage of morphine the pathologist ignored the excess morphine in the urine. He had no reason to consider any cause of death except multiple sclerosis."

Moynihan pressed on, "Am I correct in assuming, doctor, that the presence of excess morphine in the urine does not necessarily mean that the deceased died of morphine poisoning?"

In my mind's eye, I envisioned Archer sitting up in the witness chair and staring angrily at Moynihan. "This patient was not terminally ill. In multiple sclerosis, a remission may occur at any time. But twenty milligrams of morphine on top of ten, administered in a matter of minutes, would certainly cause respiratory or cardiac arrest and death."

"Is it not a fact, doctor, that this situation posed an embarrassing problem for the hospital? How could the staff permit conditions which gave Lake the opportunity to poison his wife, as you claim?"

"Objection," the record showed Traver remarking, probably shouting. "Heritage Hospital is not on trial."

Moynihan: "Your Honor, this man is the prosecution's expert witness on behalf of the hospital. I think this dual involvement has the appearance of a conflict of interest and warrants some leeway in cross examination."

Judge Whelan agreed: "Objection overruled."

The question was read back to the witness. Dr. Archer responded: "There is nothing which could have been done to stop Lake. The nurses left their station because they had to handle an emergency. They had no reason to fear that someone would take the vial of morphine and inject Mrs. Lake. There was no negligence on the part of the staff. Rather, we must look at Mr. Lake. He hounded the staff for weeks. asking for more morphine for his wife. He didn't simply suggest or ask. He was belligerent. He was a wild man. He told me he would rather see his wife dead than to have to suffer such pain, and he insisted Mrs. Lake felt the same. I told him an increased dose might kill his wife, but he still persisted. To claim or even to infer that Heritage Hospital was negligent in this matter is absolutely unjustified. And to claim that I would make a false charge because I happen to be chief of staff is nothing more than a feeble attempt to shift the blame to others."

And yet, despite Dr. Archer's testimony, the jury had acquitted Arthur Lake.

4

Although I was not opposed to having a glass of wine with dinner, I was not a habitué of bars, so it was with some temerity that I entered the Tap Room at precisely five-thirty the following day. The Tap Room was a sportman's bar—a long, dark and dismal saloon punctuated with the heads of shaggy animals and redolent of tobacco. Four television sets, one tuned to a baseball game, one devoted to ice hockey, one featuring a boxing match, and one blasting scores and replays from around the world, competed for the attention of a dozen reporters, most of whom were drunk or in spirited disagreement with one another.

I secured a booth, ordered a glass of white wine and toyed with it until six-thirty when, without apology, Harriet Owens slid into the seat opposite, plopped a manuscript and flashlight on the table and waved to the bartender who promptly brought her a cocktail. I started to say something, but she shook her head and her hair danced around her face like firelight. "Don't talk; read!"

Arthur Lake was portrayed in Harriet's manuscript as weak and easily manipulated. The picture of Martha Smith that emerged was simply brutal. According to Harriet, Martha had used her charm and wit to make herself and her lover very rich. That she had done so in less than twenty years garnered Harriet's grudging admiration. The article detailed how Martha had unscrupulously bought land which she knew had great value from poor, uninformed farmers for one-tenth the land's value. Time and again she purchased options and exercised them only when she could make ten, fifteen or twenty times her cost. Sometimes she waited until she had a commitment from others to finance a development, usually a shopping center or apartments or both. She induced rich people to provide money for development, then froze them out, acquiring developed property for herself without investing one cent. She used the clientele of Arthur Lake, accumulated over a period of many years, to promote herself and her ventures. She joined organizations to promote herself. She seduced men, wealthy men, professional men, with her beauty and her charm. They were at her feet. She and Lake would go to conferences and meetings together and register in separate rooms, but at business sessions and formal dinners they acted as though they were married and many people assumed they were.

It was a scathing attack which revealed not one redeeming feature about Martha Smith. There was only a casual mention of Arthur Lake. He was pictured as just another victim of an avaricious woman; but one who had financial reasons to marry her.

The most crushing part of the article was the report of a survey in which five hundred people were asked, "Do you think Martha Smith was involved in the murder of Hannah Lake?" Seventy percent answered "yes."

I straightened the pages and set them on the table. "You don't like Martha Smith very much do you?"

"I don't care about her one way or the other," Harriet said, spearing a cigarette from a pack and waiting for me to light it. When I failed to respond, she dug a lighter from her purse and handed it to me.

I declined. "I won't be party to your lung cancer," I said.

Furiously, she snatched the lighter from my hand, lit her cigarette, and blew smoke in my face. "A pretty strong indictment, counselor, wouldn't you say?" she asked, nodding at the manuscript.

"Who conducted the survey?" I asked, coughing.

"I did," she challenged.

"No wonder you were late getting here."

"I thought I'd give you a chance to meet some real men," she snapped.

"Compared to you, they're probably all wimps."

Unsure of whether to be pleased or insulted, she waved to a grizzled man in a fedora unsteadily heading our way. "Stan, come here. Let me introduce you to Lansing's newest and cleanest lawyer. Mark Pierce, meet Stanley Forrester, executive producer of *Inside Hollywood.*"

"A young shark, eh?" Forrester said, extending his hand. "You've come to the right school." To Harriet he said, "He's telegenic. You could use him."

"For what?" I'd heard that Harriet Owens was being touted as the new anchor for *Inside Hollywood.* A tabloid television show could rebut public opinion.

Harriet dampened my enthusiasm. "For bait," she said, derisively. "Stanley, this kid isn't a shark; he's not even a shark-in-training."

"You're right," I said, getting up and offering Stan my seat. "I'm bait, all right. Jail bait. Better ask the next kid you pick up for ID."

Forrester laughed until he coughed. Harriet snorted. I tossed a twenty on the table and said, "Have another on me," and left the bar. It was a nice gesture, but I had to eat rice and beans that night."

Delving into Martha Smith's past wasn't easy, and for days after my meeting with Harriet I was tempted to contact her to ask her for sources, but I knew she'd exact too high a price. Although Martha had not been charged, she was at the center of the story.

I studied the transcript and jotted down the names of Martha's secretary, Jessie Barden, and Arthur's secretary, Francis

Wyman. There were the names of all the nurses who had been involved as well as mention of Ted and Margie Strange and Bonnie Fisher, although no addresses were provided for them.

I drove over to the hospital first, because that was most expedient, and I interviewed Delores Winfield, the nurse in charge of the station at the time of Mrs. Lake's death. She was a brusque, middle-aged woman, six-feet tall and very solid. She told me that she had never, "Not in nearly twenty years of nursing, seen a husband carry on about his wife's condition and what should be done about it. He told me his power of attorney authorized him to change medication and he kept insisting on more morphine. When Doctor Archer told him more morphine might cause cardiac or respiratory arrest, he said his wife preferred death to agony and that he had the power to give her more morphine.

" 'Now Mister Lake,' I said, 'morphine is a powerful drug; it's a killer,' and he told me that if she should die that was all right. He said, 'I cannot watch my wife die inch by inch. It would be better if she died immediately.' Oh, he wouldn't listen to anybody. He was a wild man."

"How much morphine was prescribed," I asked her.

"Mrs. Lake had been receiving eight milligrams of morphine over a period of four hours and Doctor Archer increased it to ten milligrams, still a safe dosage. When she passed on, we all assumed it was on account of multiple sclerosis."

"Isn't it true," I asked her, "that there's a certain amount of drug pilfering that goes on?"

"Well, I wouldn't know about that. You'd have to speak with Doctor Archer."

Doctor Archer refused to confirm or deny that drugs were sometimes stolen from the pharmacy, although he said it was not unheard of. He insisted, however, that an overdose of morphine was responsible for Mrs. Lake's death. "The autopsy was confined to the brain and spinal column because the purpose of the autopsy was to determine the extent of the damage to the myelin, the protective covering of nerve fiber. We try to get and keep this information in the course of learning more about multiple sclerosis. The severity of the disease and the accompanying pain varies greatly from patient to patient. We don't know why there is this great variation. In Mrs. Lake's case there had been extensive damage to the myelin over a wide area, which accounts for her extreme pain."

"Why did it take a full week to discover that twenty-milligram vial of morphine was missing?" I asked him.

"We weigh and count narcotics weekly, unless we have reason to suspect discrepancies. Now, I really must go. Arthur Lake got away with murder. There's no use beating a dead horse." He looked at me keenly. "That was a poor choice of words; don't quote me."

I assured him I had no such intention. I was half convinced that somebody else could have administered the morphine. The more I thought about this, however, the more it became apparent that only Lake or Smith had a motive. Again, this demonstrated the difference between trial by law and trial by public opinion. In a court of law, the only question was whether there was sufficient evidence to prove beyond a reasonable doubt that the cause of death was morphine poisoning. But in the court of public opinion in which I was now practicing it was enough to convict if the defendant did not prove by at least a strong inference that somebody else committed the crime. It was becoming clear to me that I could not show by inference or otherwise that somebody else might have committed this crime.

Before leaving the hospital, I interviewed Mandy Williams, Mrs. Lake's night nurse. Mandy was a heavyset African-American woman in her late thirties with a glorious smile and an infectious laugh. She kept striking poses and looking around for the cameraman, disbelieving that I wasn't with the media. When I mentioned drugs, however, she froze, and I was only able to elicit "yes" and "no" answers until the subject of Martha Smith came up. "I understand she didn't visit Mrs. Lake very often."

"She came in the evening," Mandy said, "Real nice lady. Rachel, too."

"Who's Rachel?"

"She didn't act like any housekeeper, she was more like a friend. They were eating pecan fudge. They gave me some fudge and landsakes, that was the best fudge I ever tasted." She licked her lips. "I wouldn't mind some of that fudge about now. Rachel made it, said her momma was famous all over Memphis for that fudge."

"Did you say her last name?"

"Who?"

"Rachel."

"No, she was just a colored lady from New York."

"I thought you said she was from Memphis."

"I said her momma was from Memphis. For a TV guy, you don't listen very well, do you?"

"I'm not from TV."

"Then what I'm doing wasting my time talkin' to you for?" And with that, Mandy Williams walked away, looking this way and that for the cameraman she hoped to find, licking her lips at the memory of pecan fudge.

I next called upon a doctor who was acquainted with the case of People v. Lake but had not been called to testify. Dr. Russell Longworth lived in Grand Ledge, ten miles away. I asked him, "At what volume does morphine become lethal?"

"That depends on other factors—the general health of the patient and whether the patient has developed a tolerance for it. Tolerance can be acquired in as little as two weeks. In such cases it will take a larger dose to make it lethal. Ordinarily in intravenous use eight to fifteen milligrams are safe. There are moderate toxic effects in intravenous dosage of twenty to thirty milligrams. Serious side effects can result in dosages over thirty milligrams. Sensitivity to morphine varies greatly among adults. Where there is high sensitivity, fifteen milligrams could cause deep coma. In the Lake case, as I have been told, there was no evidence of high sensitivity. Usually we try to use five to ten milligrams over a period of three to four hours. We are pretty sure we will have no trouble in that range."

"Suppose, however," I asked, "the patient is getting ten milligrams every four hours and suddenly he or she gets an additional twenty milligrams in a matter of minutes?"

"I would say that could very well cause respiratory arrest and death."

I thanked Dr. Longworth for his time and drove to Okemos, an upper class but moderate town where Martha Smith lived in a sedate brick townhouse on a couple of well-manicured acres. Security guards were at the gate keeping half a dozen reporters at bay, admitting no one. I signaled to a lanky African-American guard and asked him if Rachel was with Mrs. Smith.

"Rachel Strong?"

"Yes. I think she's Mrs. Smith's housekeeper."

"I wouldn't know about that," he said.

"Older woman," I said, "light-colored African-American. Makes great pecan fudge."

"That's Rachel Strong all right, but she's no housekeeper. Maybe she was once upon a time, but she has no need to work any more. She's almost as rich as Martha Smith."

"Does she live here, too?" I asked, noticing that we had drawn the attention of the other uniformed guard and a cop in plainclothes.

"Now, that's none of your business, is it? What do you want with Rachel?"

"What's going on here, Freddy?" the plainclothes cop asked.

"Nothing," Fred said. "He's not asking about Mrs. Smith."

"I don't care who he's asking about. You don't know anything!" A vein in his forehead throbbed.

"That's just what I was telling him, Mr. Stoat."

"That's what he said," I agreed, and walked back to where I'd parked my car.

Rachel Strong was not listed in the phone book. I didn't know anyone at the phone company who'd research unlisted numbers for me, so I called Roxanne Weber, the meter maid who'd given me a ticket and asked her if she'd check drivers' licenses for Rachel Strong. "What's it worth to you?" she laughed.

"What would you like?"

"A man with imagination," she teased. "A Porsche. Season tickets to the baseball games."

"How about dinner?"

"At a nice restaurant," Roxanne insisted. "Not some pizza joint."

"I'll let you pick the place," I offered.

"What happened to men with imagination?"

"They got out of Lansing as fast as they could."

"I'll call you," Roxanne said and hung up.

5

While waiting to hear from Roxanne, it occurred to me that I might get something out of questioning the jury. After all, it was their verdict.

I found in the Lake court file that the jury foreman in the Lake case was Louis Marchant. His number was listed, and he agreed to come to my office the following morning. This I had not expected, and I hastily phoned my on-call receptionist, Sally Farris, and also arranged to have the office dusted so my lack of clients would not be altogether apparent.

A wiry man who perspired freely, Mr. Louis Marchant was a CPA with the firm of Drexel, Berger and Marchant. "I was wondering why nobody contacted me or the other members of the jury," he said, wiping his brow with a large white handkerchief. "The media has been beating on us pretty heavy, especially that reporter from the *Exposé Magazine,* Harriet Owens. Everybody thinks Lake was guilty, but nobody asked us why we acquitted him. Do you have something to drink? It's hot in here."

"Just water," I said.

"Water's fine," Marchant said. "You got any ice?"

"I'll see what we can do," I said, summoning Sally. She came in with a notepad, which was a nice touch but wholly unnecessary, especially since she didn't take shorthand.

"I can get some Cokes at the coffee shop," she suggested.

"Well here is your chance, Mr. Marchant," I said when Sally had gone. "Tell me how you arrived at your decision to acquit."

"We disposed of this case very quickly," he said, wiping his forehead. "We were unanimous from the beginning. There was not one, but two very serious doubts about Mr. Lake's guilt. First, the testimony on which the prosecution rested their case was that of Doctor Archer. There was no testimony at all about putting morphine into the victim. And Archer's testimony was weak. His testimony that the defendant had administered twenty milligrams of morphine was sheer conjecture. You attorneys depend on conjecture; we jurors consider circumstances but we must be convinced beyond a reasonable doubt as to what those circumstances prove. Doctor Archer was a very good witness. We accepted what he had to say. But the crux of his case rested on three milligrams of free morphine in Hannah Lake's urine. Archer said it was accepted medical practice to calculate the residue as ten percent of the intake. But there is a difference between medical practices and legal proof.

"If that three milligrams in the urine was medical proof that thirty milligrams had been given, why did the autopsy report not say that the deceased died of morphine poisoning? Obviously the medical staff was not willing to put that into the record. They wrote that she had died of multiple sclerosis. Second, there was no evidence of when the vial of morphine actually disappeared. It was a week after this incident had occurred before it was missed. But it could have disappeared the day before or the week before Mrs. Lake's death. One witness testified that the vial could have disappeared long before she died.

"Under these circumstances, the jury had no reason to give consideration to the alleged love affair. Certainly we could not possibly decide that because Lake loved Smith, Lake must have administered morphine to kill his wife. Particularly when we didn't have the evidence to prove she died of morphine poisoning."

Sally arrived with drinks for all of us. I set mine aside and watched Marchant's Adam's apple bob up and down as he drank. When he finished, he wiped his face and took up his train of thought. "I am not a lawyer," he said. "But as a layman I cannot help but see the irony in this case. The jury could not get to the love affair because there was not enough proof of the administration of morphine, but the public starts with the love affair and jumps to the conclusion that the defendant did administer the morphine with intent to kill his wife."

"Well," I countered, "the public doesn't necessarily make that leap. It just wonders and expresses its curiosity on a daily basis."

Marchant was so disgusted, he spat into his handkerchief. "The public wants its pound of flesh," he said. "The uproar is deafening. I feel sorry for the acquitted, and for his family. It may be the price of freedom but it's a hell of a price to pay."

I pushed my Coke over to him and watched him drink. "I think so, too," I said.

"And we jurors are also being denigrated, if not personally, then as a group. I'm sure it will affect my company's bottom line, but I stand by the decision I was instrumental in reaching. I'm sure we were right. Doctor Archer made it clear that a medical standard is not necessarily an absolute. It is an estimate, an approximation, which generally is sufficient for most purposes—but as proof of murder? Never!"

Marchant had worked himself up to such a state that he was drenched in perspiration. I watched with horror as he swabbed his face with the handkerchief into which he had recently expectorated. "I appreciate your concern," I said, pushing a box of Kleenex across the desk.

He grabbed a handful, shoved the tissues into his pocket, and extracted a business card. "When you're ready," he said. "No pressure. The money you save in taxes often covers our cost. Shall we discuss it over lunch?" He waited for me to say something.

The phone rang and I ducked the invitation. Sally showed him out while I greeted Roxanne enthusiastically. "I was thinking of Cicero's but you sound so happy to hear from me maybe I should choose that little French restaurant in Okemos."

"You located Rachel Strong?"

"She lives in Okemos, too," Roxanne said, and I grabbed pencil and paper and copied down the address she gave me which turned out to be Martha's address.

"After paying my parking fine, I can barely afford Cicero's," I said. "Thursday night?"

"Pick me up at seven. Do you know where I live?"

"Remind me."

Roxanne gave me her address and I wrote it down. "I live with my parents," she said. "Don't honk your horn. Park your car and ring the bell."

"What kind of animals do you go out with?" I asked.

"I'll find out tomorrow," she laughed.

The next morning I drove to Okemos, which is a suburb of Lansing, and called on Rachel Strong. A tall, slender woman in her sixties, opened the door and asked what I wanted.

"Some fudge," I said. "Pecan fudge. I hear you make the best fudge in town."

"Who told you that?" she laughed.

"Someone who knows good fudge."

She studied me carefully, decided I looked harmless enough, and invited me in. "There's nothing like Memphis fudge," she said to me. "Wait right here and I'll get some for you."

"You can't be from Memphis," I said. "You don't have a Southern accent."

"Well, I lived for many years in New York."

"My name is Mark Pierce."

She shook my hand. "Rachel Strong," she said, "wait here." She left, returning minutes later with a white paper bag containing caramel-colored fudge laced with pecans."

"Does Martha Smith live there?" I asked.

"Yes. In this house. You are in my apartment in Martha's house."

"Is she from Memphis, too?"

"Oh, no, she's from Breckenridge."

"Michigan?"

"Yes . . . " She clapped her mouth with her hand. "You're the second one tricked me like that. Who told you about my momma's fudge? That newslady?"

"What newslady?" I asked. "Harriet Owens?"

"I'm not saying another word. You get out of here now. Go on, scat!"

"This is excellent fudge," I said. "I haven't . . . "

"I'm sure you haven't. Now, git!"

Paperbag in hand, I backed out the door. "I'm sorry," I said and shamefacedly turned away.

"Hmmph!" she grunted and slammed the door.

6

Breckenridge is a small town of about a thousand people sixty miles north of Lansing. It was famous in a small way as the birthplace of Jimmy Smith, All-American running back, twice an all-pro, most recently miscast as Pat Garrett in the umpteenth remake of Billy the Kid, according to the article I had read in the *Detroit News.* The reviewer gave it half a star, two-thumbs down, but reserved his harshest criticism for the football hero turned matinee idol. "A western without direction starring a hero without a clue," wrote the reviewer. "As wooden as a Yucca, which is all this writer can say about Jimmy Smith's latest affront to the acting profession."

I rented a Ford Export and drove north (on U.S. 27). A thriving agricultural area, it was quiet—not a place of adventure or nightlife.

I had no idea how to proceed, so I walked around town showing Martha Smith's picture to everyone over fifty I bumped into. Anyone younger would have no idea who she was, since she'd lived in Ann Arbor, Michigan for only a few years and in New York after that, as I was to learn. In the local supermarket, two silver-haired ladies, their hair in nets, told me Martha Smith was born Martha Toller, but when I showed them my picture of Martha they fell silent. "That's not Ida's girl," one said. "We're sorry. Smith is such a common name."

"What happened to her," I asked. "Ida's daughter Martha?"

"They got married, certainly," replied the silver-haired lady whose name badge read Louise Varnum. "Although there was some talk."

"It was hushed up after the divorce," confided her associate, "if there was a divorce."

"Mona Wilson, for shame! There was marriage and a divorce, certainly."

"To whom?" I asked.

The silver-haired ladies looked at one another, then at me. "Why, to Jimmy Smith, certainly," said Louise Varnum. "Although no one could understand why he married such a homely girl."

"If he did marry her," Mona Wilson intoned.

At the Register of Records in the courthouse in Ithaca, the county seat, I confirmed the births of Jimmy Smith and, a few months later, Martha Toller. I showed the office workers the picture of Martha Smith. "Since she's a national figure, if she grew up in these parts someone must remember her," I explained.

"That's not the Martha Smith I know," said Sunday Mathers, the register of deeds. "That Martha Smith is the mistress of Arthur Lake. I read all about her in the *Free Press.* But she is not the girl who was born and raised here."

It was frustrating. I pointed to the phone. "This is the Martha Smith of the Lake case, but I believe that she was born here. Does the name Rachel Strong mean anything to you?"

"Strom?"

"Strong. An African-American woman of about fifty."

Sunday Mathers shook his head. "The only colored family in these parts go by the name of Hutchison. They kept pretty much to their kind, so they'd know about the Strom gal you're looking for. But if you're talking about the Martha Smith who made all the headlines, she's not the Martha Smith who grew up in Breckenridge, no sir. The Martha Smith we knew was no beauty. She is definitely not the woman in this here picture."

"There could have been two Martha Smiths," I said, more to myself than Mathers.

The Registrar acknowledged the possibility, "That's a very common name. There are probably thousands of Martha Smiths in the United States. What I can tell you is that the Martha Smith you are talking about is not Martha Toller Smith. Our Martha was no beauty. She was pleasant, and she had a pretty face, but she weighed at least a hundred seventy-five pounds, and her nose was too big for her face. This picture is of a woman with a good figure. Martha's figure was not a good one. And she paid no attention to the clothes she wore. She was not a good dresser."

I took my hand from my still-peeling nose. "But she could have changed over the years."

"Well, lots of things can happen in twenty years, but a leopard doesn't change its spots. I haven't seen Martha Toller since high school, but I didn't give her a second look back then and I never could figure out what Jim Smith saw in her. Matter of fact, I never thought much of him. Light-headed but fast as the wind. Couldn't tie his shoes without a woman swooning over him. You know what's wrong with this country?"

"We have fools for heroes?" I guessed.

"Yer darn tooting," said Sunday Mathers.

I didn't ask him how he got his name. I assumed he was born on the Sabbath. I did not visit Breckenridge High, where Jimmy Smith's trophies gleamed within glass cases. I was tired of the cloying gossip of small-town America. Perhaps I was jealous of the local hero. I'd been backup quarterback in my senior year for a winless Princeton team—no trophies, no spoils, no adoring fans.

Unable to find a single person to confirm Martha Smith's identity, I drove home to Lansing. That evening as I was about to undress and climb into bed the phone started ringing.

It was Sally Farris, my occasional secretary. "Where have you been?" she asked. "I've been calling for hours."

"I'm sorry," I said, feeling guilty for no good reason. "What's up?"

"Mister Tim Moynihan, Arthur Lake's defense attorney, you know?

"Yes, yes."

"Well, I don't know how he got my phone number, but he told me to locate you and tell you to be at his office at ten o'clock this morning."

"What for?"

"He wouldn't say, but I'm sure it has to do with the Lake case."

"Thank you, Sally. I'm sorry to have been the cause of your not sleeping."

"That's all right, Mr. Pierce. I will get paid for the day, won't I? Mr. Moynihan said I would."

"He did, did he?"

"I really need the money, Mr. Pierce."

"You'll get paid, Sally. Now go to sleep."

"Thank you, Mr. Pierce. Good night."

At nine-thirty in the morning, I entered Tim Moynihan's office. "You're early," he said. "The others won't get there until ten."

"What others?"

"Arthur Lake and Martha Smith."

"That's interesting," I observed. "The last time I talked to you, you didn't want me to go near them."

Moynihan leaned on his desk as he faced me. "Things are different now. We have a horrible problem. Ironically, I think you can help us with that problem as you go about investigating the Lake case."

This was more than a surprise. It was a shock. How could this be? I kept my composure. I was not sure about Moynihan at this point. His statement was so far-fetched that he must have had some sinister work to be done and I was his choice of fall guy. "Well, let's have it," I blurted out.

"Let's wait for Lake and Smith," Moynihan retorted. At that moment Mr. Lake and Mrs. Smith and Rachel Strong walked into the room.

Moynihan took over. "Art and Martha, as I told you I have Mr. Mark Pierce here and I want him to help us. He can do it easier than we can help ourselves. He is independent and he is trying to rewrite the story of the Lake case. Now, Mr. Pierce, we will tell you something I have refused to tell you before this moment. Mrs. Smith here is the former wife of Jimmy Smith, Hollywood heart-throb and former All-American, All-Pro football player." He hesitated. This was my second shock since entering this office only moments before. This answered the basic question to which I had tried so hard to find an answer. But this Martha Smith was no fat, ugly lady. She was a beauty. Then came the next shock—bigger than the others. "As you have read, Mrs. Smith is the mother of Michelle Morgan, movie star. Michelle Morgan is dating the great Jimmy Smith who is her father!"

"Wow!" I exploded.

"Our problem, Mr. Pierce, is that Mrs. Harriet Owens is engaged in what she calls investigative reporting and, sooner or later, she will learn about this ridiculous affair, and that would probably ruin Michelle's career."

"Wait a minute," I interrupted. "How is it possible that a father and daughter are dating? That's too absurd to be believed."

"They don't know they are father and daughter," Moynihan answered calmly.

"They don't know?" I exclaimed. And I didn't express some nasty thought which lurked in my mind.

"However absurd this may sound it is the truth. Jimmy Smith divorced Martha when Martha was pregnant with Michelle and Melinda. She announced at the divorce proceeding that she was pregnant but Jimmy Smith never saw her again and never inquired about any child or about her condition. And she refused to tell him what he should have asked her. So, now we have this mess on our hands."

"And what do you want me to do?"

"We want you to tell Michelle of her predicament."

"Why me?"

"You, because you have the best entree. You can go to her for an interview about her mother. She probably knows what you are doing and if she doesn't know you can tell her when you make the appointment?"

"Why can't Martha do it?" I saw no reason why I should be drawn into this. Moynihan answered: "We do not want a confrontation. That's what it would be if Martha tried to tell her daughter. If you have talked to Mrs. Strong you know what Martha went through. You can explain that to Michelle and it will make Michelle understand. Martha cannot tell her daughter the whole story."

I turned to Mrs. Strong. This time she seemed receptive.

"We will be glad to pay you for your efforts," Mr. Lake added.

"What will you be paying me for?" I asked.

"To save my daughter's life," Martha put in.

"It means a lot to us," Arthur Lake continued. "We will gladly pay you ten thousand dollars."

"I'm sure Mr. Moynihan can tell you that I cannot take your money. I'm not for sale. And I don't want to spoil my work by the taint of money."

Moynihan said nothing. A period of silence followed. In that time my thoughts went back to Lansing's Eastern High School and Michelle Smith, now Michelle Morgan, movie star.

My crush on her was still strong. In fact I was beginning to see this as an opportunity to do what I had been afraid to do as a teenager. That was the only reason I was considering not the money but the opportunity to win her over—for her mother and maybe for me.

Moynihan was not finished. "So far as we know this Owens gal knows nothing about Jimmy Smith. She knows Martha has two children but she has not found their birth records. She has been to Breckenridge and to Ithaca, the county seat for Gratiot County, where she found Martha's birth record. She had no reason to check Jimmy Smith's birth record and the children were not born in Breckenridge or in Michigan. We have an opportunity to break the news to Michelle before she reads it in the newspapers."

"Can't you get an injunction or restraining order?" Lake asked.

"No," Moynihan responded. "First, we cannot allege or prove the information is false and second, a court is not likely to enjoin free speech. And even if we could do that it would be the best way to tell our secret to the whole world."

I was sure that Harriet Owens would do anything to learn everything about Martha Smith. I was sure she would find a record of the divorce in Ann Arbor and the provision in it that the husband would pay support money for an expected child. That would drive her on to the limit.

I still had a question. "Informing Michelle will be the easy part of the problem. What can be done to simply block the information, wipe it out?" I got no immediate suggestion.

Next I asked: "What about Jimmy Smith? Do we tell him he has two beautiful daughters, one of whom he is currently courting? Do we have a responsibility to advise him?" Again silence. Moynihan finally took the challenge. "If we tell her but don't tell him we have lost control of the situation. We have merely muddied the waters. We have no way of knowing what will happen next. What does she tell him when he asks for a date? 'I mustn't go out with you because you are my father.' We can't leave that burden on her. We must talk to both of them."

Martha visibly winced when she heard Moynihan's words. She said nothing.

Moynihan went on, "As for stopping Owens, there is nothing that can be done. All we can do is immediately stop the affair between Smith and his daughter and hope that a long time passes before Owens learns the truth—long enough so it won't be news anymore."

"One more question," I requested, "I must know who is the real Martha Smith. That question may be strange but I have reason to ask the question."

Moynihan smiled broadly. "Mr. Pierce, there is only one Martha Smith. She is here in this room and she comes from Breckenridge. Why she looks different is another story for which we have no time today. I assume you will go to Los Angeles, for that is where Jimmy and Michelle live. I'll buy your ticket, first class, return too."

With that the meeting adjourned. As I drove home I pondered my new adventure. It appeared to me that the only safe thing to do was to speak to Jimmy and Michelle at the same time in the same place. This question brought me to the disturbing realization that I had agreed to do something for which I was utterly unprepared. What could I tell these two people to help them in such a terrible situation? I simply did not know enough about the background. Jimmy and Michelle would know immediately that their relationship must end. But what would be the consequence of such an end? It would be almost cruel simply to say: "You cannot continue your affair because you are father and daughter!" Of course it would be easy for me to say that the consequences were not my responsibility but theirs. But was it? How were they to blame? It all came back to Martha.

This was her doing. Not exactly! Jimmy had something to do with it.

Were there any mitigating circumstances which would at least in part, alleviate the wrong Martha had committed? I had reason to believe there were such circumstances. Martha's struggles would explain her action—not excuse it, just explain it. Although I had worked on the case for a week, I did not yet have all of the details of her travail at hand. In lieu of her rapid rise, there must have been a rags-to-riches story.

There was not time to cover all this ground as it should be covered. Owens was out to destroy not only Martha but Jimmy and Michelle as well. She was a good reporter, almost vicious in her determination. It was imperative that I talk to these two people as soon as possible.

I had another problem. What in the world was I doing to this mess? What did this have to do with the death of Hannah Lake? Here the parameters of my so-called investigation came into focus. In a court of law all of this would be irrelevant. In the court of public opinion everything was relevant insofar as it helped fill out the picture of the people involved.

I took an afternoon flight to Los Angeles, reached there in the early evening. It was too late to do anything. The next morning I called Mr. Harman, Jimmy Smith's agent, and told him that Jimmy Smith's and Michelle Morgan's careers could be ruined and that I must talk to Jimmy as well as Michelle. I got Michelle's agents name from Harman and called him. Both were wary of me but they could not take any chances with their clients' careers so it was arranged that the five of us, Jimmy and Michelle and Harman and Marshall Richardson, of Richardson & Associates, Michelle's agent, and myself would meet at Harman's office at three o'clock the afternoon of the day I had talked to Richardson.

I asked Jimmy and Michelle to sit next to their respective agents and the twosome to be about ten feet apart in the front of Harman's desk at which I sat.

"I'm Mark Pierce of Lansing, Michigan," I began when I was interrupted by Michelle. "Mark Pierce, you were in high school with Melinda and me, in the same class."

"That's right," I replied. "I didn't think you would remember me."

"How could anyone forget the handsome guy, six feet tall who was called 'straight arrow' because he never used any swear word, and who never dated."

I'm afraid I blushed terribly. In fact I was shocked. This girl I hadn't had the courage to ask for a date now spoke as though she might have welcomed my invitation. She was simply being nice!

I continued my operation. "Jimmy Smith," I said to the big movie star, thinking that to call him 'Jimmy' would cause aggravation, "you don't know me. Let me tell you something about myself. I've just started a one-man law firm in Lansing where I was born and have lived all my life. I've been entranced by the Lake murder trial and am trying to get behind the news stories and learn that what really happened. In doing that I discovered that the Martha Smith in the Lake case is Martha Toller Smith of Breckenridge, Michigan and the famous Martha Smith is your former wife whom you divorced many years ago in Ann Arbor, Michigan, while you were attending the university. Michelle Smith-Morgan and Melinda Smith-Trudeau are your and Martha's twin daughters."

It was Harman who spoke up: "What kind of a game is this? Whatever it is, it's a dangerous game for you, Mr. Pierce. Jimmy Smith has no children and you are not going to foist a couple on him. I don't get it. This is absurd."

Marshall Richardson said nothing, he was all ears.

I became lawyer-like.

"Let's start at the beginning. Do you admit you married and divorced Martha Toller?"

"Just a minute!" It was Harman again. "We didn't come here for an inquisition."

I kept my ground. "I told you, Mr. Harman, that your client's career is at stake in this matter. You thought it worthwhile to hear me out. That's why we are here. If you have changed your mind, you and your client may leave."

Harman now blushed. "I know your kind. You will get a statement that will incriminate Mr. Smith. You are probably wired to record whatever he says. We won't fall into that trap."

"Very well, then, just leave and take your client with you."

"And that would suit your purposes completely, wouldn't it! In our absence you might catch Michelle in some double meaning statement which you could sell for a lot of money."

"Very well, then, stay!"

Now Harman was almost out of control. "I'm telling my client to answer no more questions."

"And you won't ask questions," I shot back.

"I'll do whatever I want. You are not my boss or my keeper."

I decided to turn to Michelle expecting to hear Richardson complain. He didn't complain. He said very simply: "You have already stated your claim that Jimmy and Michelle are father and daughter. We know Michelle is Martha Smith's daughter. You have brought into this scene another Martha Smith. Or, at least, she appears to be another Martha Smith. It's your job to prove what you claim. It is not for us to make your case for you." He was soft spoken.

"You are not getting it," I replied with some force, "I'm not here to prove anything. I'm here to tell you that a big story is about to break which will be very harmful to your clients and something must be done to offset the blow. Are you insisting on doing nothing and have the world know that Jimmy Smith is courting his own daughter? What point would there be for me to fabricate such a possibility? I'm not going to write such a story. Be real!"

"Okay, Mr. Smart guy, what do we do?" Harman had quieted down a bit.

"Tomorrow," I answered, "will be the Academy Awards. Jimmy and Michelle should go with different parties. And thereafter they must continue doing the same. That will take the wind out of the *Exposé* story."

Now Michelle spoke up. "And how do you propose that I find another escort?"

Alas, my opportunity, "I would be most happy to escort you."

Michelle had not expected this. Richardson picked up the idea. "That's a great idea," he said. "That will avoid another embarrassment. Jimmy, why don't you ask Rita LeClair? She has acted with you and she would be glad to go with you."

"If she doesn't already have a date." Harman was still very skeptical.

"Call her now," I suggested. He did. She agreed to go when Jimmy explained that he was not taking Michelle and needed a companion for the evening.

At that moment I had another shock. Harman's secretary came in. "There is a Rachel Strong here. She knows about this conference and she thinks she should be part of it!" Without being asked Rachel Strong walked past the secretary and into the midst of people now in a state of wonderment.

"I thought you would need me in these discussions. So, I've come out here. There are some aspects in this matter which you should consider and I don't think you have. Martha Smith saved my life. She is my dearest friend. She has suffered enough. I've been a witness to her struggle to keep her family alive. Nothing should be done which will hurt her more. As for Michelle, I've talked to her long ago. She knows what sacrifices her mother has made for her and Melinda because I told her.

She knows her mother has always loved her dearly. I think we should ask some questions of Mr. Harman and Mr. Richardson before you take any more steps. After all, they have been the guardians of Jimmy and Michelle for several years. They have been closer to each of them than any of us have. I'd like to ask them a question. Did you or either or both of you have anything to do with Jimmy and Michelle dating?"

This was really out of the blue. What in the world would cause this lady to pose such a question? Harman did not hesitate. "We started it, Richardson and I. We told our clients it was in their best interest to be seen together. I needed young companionship for Smith because he was forty-two and losing his bobbysoxer following and a twenty-year-old companion might cause youth to rub off on him in the eyes of his fans. Marshall needed a mature companion for Michelle because she appeared so young he could not get more mature parts for her."

"So what?" Marshall Richardson put in.

"So," Rachel responded, "this was not a spontaneous romance in which these two people romantically had found each other. It was a contrived relationship, arranged by the respective agents of the so-called lovers."

Before anybody else could speak, Jimmy Smith left his chair and went to Michelle. While she was seated and he was standing, he put his arm around her. "No matter how this all started, we became very fond of each other. But we never became intimate. She is not only young, she is completely innocent. It was inconceivable that I would ever try to be intimate with her. Thank God, I never tried. And you guys may think what you like but I love this girl more than ever right now and she must know it!"

At this point I simply exclaimed aloud: "My God."

As Smith tried to pull away from Michelle she clung to his hand. "Don't leave me," she said.

"I'll never leave you," was his reply. "We will see this through. We have nothing to be ashamed of. We were putting on an act and we got into it more than we had intended. We still love each other and I'm so proud of you!"

Rachel Strong continued: "And you two must know that Martha Smith is a courageous, loving woman who has spent a lifetime taking care of her family and her friends. If it is the last thing I do I'll see to it that the world learns the truth. For I was saved by her love."

I had not known Rachel Strong. I wanted very much to know her now. She obviously knew the whole story. She must know who killed Hannah Lake or had a good idea who had done it.

7

I rented a new tuxedo for the biggest affair I had ever or would ever attend, the night of the Oscars! Michelle arranged a limousine for me to pick her up and take her to the theatre. I was overwhelmed!

As Michelle and I seated ourselves in the car she began talking. She was a different person. She began by getting close to me after I had seated myself and took my arm. "Now, you listen to me carefully," she admonished. "I have a plan for the evening. If it works my worries are over. But you must play your part. Tonight you are my fiancé. It is the first time you have been with me in Hollywood because you have been trying to start a law practice while I have been trying to become an actress. But we have been friends since high school and have been engaged for two years! We have tried to keep our relationship secret because my father and I were using each other to help our respective careers, as our agents had planned. Not even our agents were aware that we are father and daughter.

"There will be a lot of newsmen at this blast. We will get the attention of one of them and break this story. That will stop whoever is trying to humiliate me and my father. We will break the news. There will be no hidden scandal. Got the idea?"

I am sure my mouth was wide open. This was no juvenile novice. This was another Martha Smith. She was a chip off the old block. Not even Martha could have dreamed up such a scenario. I was speechless. Before I could say anything she patted my shoulder. "You will have done all mother expected you to do and more. You will have done your job. I hope you don't mind being my fiancé for three or four hours!" In a few moments I was able to regain my senses. I saw the humorous side of all of this. "And how," I asked, "will you terminate our engagement?"

"I've thought about that," she replied. "There will be no need to rush that. We can just go on acting like we are engaged for months, maybe years. Do you object?"

"Oh, no," I managed to answer, feeling, really, that this was indeed a great evening for me.

I had real problems with this role-playing. It was more than that for me. Even with the very brief contact I had had with this girl who was once the girl of my dreams, I had become infatuated all over again but with greater regard for one who had become a very intelligent and sophisticated person. Was she still a sweet girl? I could not create a confrontation at the moment. I could not say to her: "I can't play this role. I'm afraid I love you." That might blow the whole thing. I decided I must play the game but with my own agenda in mind.

We emerged from the limo and into a crowd of many celebrities. There were others who were not celebrities, especially the media. Cameras were clicking and newspapermen were trying to reach various famous people to talk to them. Michelle nudged me toward a tall bald man who was obviously trying to approach us. She pretended she did not see the man and I followed meekly. At some distance, the man spoke to us. "Good evening, Miss Morgan," he opened.

"Good evening Mr. Monroe," she responded. Then she turned to me. "This is Mr. Harold Monroe of the *Los Angeles Times*." To him she said "This is Mark Pierce, my fiancé."

For a moment Mr. Monroe was startled. He tried not to show his shock. He turned to me, "I'm very happy to meet you."

Before he could say more, Michelle went on, "I'm really celebrating tonight."

"So I notice," Monroe said in anticipation of learning more. "I thought I saw Jimmy Smith out here with Rita LeClair. Have you two broken up?"

Michelle was now in full form. She let out a silent laugh. "Jimmy Smith and I will never break up!" Monroe was startled and so was I. "Jimmy Smith is my father!"

"Your father!" This time Monroe was no reporter, he was a bewildered man. "But . . . " he stammered, not knowing what to say at this point.

Michelle went on, "He wanted to make me better known. He is the heart-throb of all women. If I was with him often I would be better known as the envy of every woman in the country."

"But why have you kept all of this a secret?" A fair question by Monroe.

Again Michelle, put on an 'all-knowing' smile. "If everybody knew Jimmy Smith was taking his daughter out it would soon be the talk of the town that Jimmy is over the hill and devotes his time to his daughter. And it would not have done me any good. I would be Jimmy Smith's little girl, forced to go out with her father instead of a 'beau.' "

Immediately I thought, *What a fantastic performance!* This girl is just as sharp as her mother. The public would be shocked for a week or two but the threat of a scandalous, incestuous relationship had been avoided.

But Monroe persisted. "Why are you quitting your little game now?"

Michelle was equal to the challenge. "Because Mark and I have decided to be together more."

The *Los Angeles Times* ran the story as a feature in its Sunday edition—about how a devoted father went to such lengths to help the career of his twenty-one-year-old daughter. It was, of course, a shocker. There were many comments about going a bit too far to seek publicity. That was mild, indeed, compared to what might have been.

My experience in California was bizarre. I cannot find a more appropriate description. The job I had been asked to do was simply to apprise Jimmy Smith and Michelle Morgan of the impending disaster; it was not expected that we would abort the news. Yet, that is precisely what had happened—the terrible secret affair between Jimmy and his own daughter had been ended, and with no perceptible impact on the two careers! But I had not done that. Michelle had done it. I was nothing more than a prop in the program of obliteration.

I had another problem now, namely my instant engagement to the girl of my dreams, but with the caveat that the engagement must end one day. It was intended solely as a convenience useful in achieving a goal. That goal was now reached and there was no longer any need for me! How soon would I become disengaged? As I thought about this unhappy prospect I concluded that Michelle could not dispose of me that fast. If she did it would become obvious that the original assumption that in fact she and her father had indulged in an incestuous affair would reemerge stronger than ever.

I had time to salvage the engagement! I must find some way to do that. Meanwhile I remained in California temporarily in order to sustain the trick we had pulled on the media. Moynihan thought I had done a great job. I had to tell him I had done nothing. Michelle was the mastermind.

I suggested to Michelle that we should be seen together a little more often. She agreed. It was on one of these dates while we were having some coffee after a movie that she said to me: "After all these years at last I am dating you, even though it is part of what we might call a cover-up."

"You put me to shame," I told her. "I was afraid to ask you for a date while we were in high school and now I am dating the same girl but she is now a movie star."

She put down the cup of coffee she held. "Really, the pleasure is mine, Mark. It is so nice to be with somebody who is an old acquaintance. I can be myself. I don't have to be nice with somebody who has motives of his own and really doesn't care about me as a person. I'm having a problem adjusting myself to a man who has just become my father but having you around is very helpful. I'm sure you have other things to do elsewhere. I appreciate having you here with me."

"It's trite for me to say the pleasure is mine but these words really tell it all for me. I've loved you from afar for many years."

Now she laughed. "Come on, Mark, you don't have to put it on that heavy."

"I'm warning you," I said with a broad grin, "I intend to take full advantage of this strange circumstance. You will have to keep me around for a while because if you throw me out soon everybody will have caught on to your plan to use me as a decoy. You must make our affair look real and I will help by making it real."

From her looks at this point I could see that she would not be displeased if I played my part for real. That was encouraging.

Suddenly my beautiful date turned serious.

"Just what are you doing about the so-called Lake case? We would like it to go away. That is, Melinda, Mother, Art, Rachel,—everybody. But you insist on keeping it alive. I don't want any part of that. You had better understand that right now."

"Then, you are willing to see Martha and Art pilloried every day of the year! You believe they are innocent. Yet you will do nothing to help clear their names. Is that what I am to conclude?"

"That's not what I want. I just think it is best to let time clear their names."

"That may never happen." I suggested, trying to speak authoritatively. As I spoke those words I began to think I was choosing at this point to justify both Arthur Lake's behavior and the conduct indulged in by the two of them.

Michelle was still adamant. "Just how are you going to get at the truth? My mother is helpless. And anything Arthur Lake might say would simply snowball this wretched business."

I now had the solution to the mystery which had stumped me for so long. There was only one Martha Smith. Jimmy Smith was her divorced husband. Michelle and Melinda were their children.

But all of this was a subject, a story within a story, interesting, fascinating. What did it have to do with my basic mystery: Did Arthur Lake kill his wife?

8

Because Moynihan was anxious to apprise Michelle and Jimmy of the potential crisis which Harriet Owens was about to bring about with her story; events moved quickly. Within three weeks of the date of the verdict, Michelle's maneuver had forestalled the story pertaining to her relation with her father. All were greatly relieved. Alas, the relief did not last long. Moynihan called Lake and Martha as well as myself and we were asked to come to his office as soon as possible. We each agreed to be in his office the very next day.

As often happened with me, I was about ten minutes late for the meeting. As I entered the office I saw Arthur Lake, Martha Smith, and Rachel Strong. I took the only empty chair. It was obvious nothing had transpired before my arrival.

Moynihan spoke directly to me. "I believe you told me that you talked to the foreman of the jury on our lawsuit. Is that right?"

I acknowledged that I had spoken to Mr. Marchant about the jury's verdict.

"Apparently," Moynihan went on, "you were not the only one who talked to Mr. Marchant. Mr. Traver did the same thing. Mr. Traver got a written statement from Mr. Marchant and then talked to every member of the jury. They all signed a statement that they never considered, in their deliberation, the matter of the love affair between Arthur Lake and Martha Smith. If I remember correctly that's precisely what you had been told."

"That's right," I replied.

"Well," Mr. Moynihan continued, "Mr. Traver got affidavits from each juror and based on those affidavits has filed a motion for a new trial because the jury did not even consider the affair."

I was shocked. Rarely does the prosecution ask for a new trial when one is acquitted. I didn't know what to say. The others let out gasps of astonishment, not fully understanding.

"Mr. Traver claims that the record was full of circumstantial evidence and that compelled the jury to consider motives. He says in his motion: 'Where there is circumstantial evidence it is the obligation of a jury to determine if the defendant had motives which would sustain the circumstantial evidence, that it is not necessary to obtain direct proof of the crime before considering the effect of possible motives, that is if there is direct proof, there is no need to consider motives. But where circumstances point in a certain direction, the jury, by it's oath, must consider the motives of the accused in passing judgment of guilt or innocence.' "

Moynihan continued to address me. "Doesn't that sound like a correct statement of the law?"

I was on the defensive. "Since when has it been the right of the court to determine what a jury must consider in its deliberations? The jury heard the testimony on the affair between Lake and Smith. They had a right to give it very little or no weight. To allow a new trial in this case would be to violate the defendants constitutional protection against double jeopardy. He cannot be tried twice for the same crime."

Moynihan looked at me with fatherly countenance. "Doesn't a jury have to follow the law in the deliberations. Can it actually ignore the law? The twelve of them admitted under oath that they deliberately refused to consider motives because the crime had not been proven by other, direct evidence. That is not the law."

I countered: "Even if there was error in that regard, still that is not justification for a new trial. Courts have repeatedly said that even in the face of error a defendant cannot be retired after a verdict of not guilty."

At this point Lake interrupted. "I don't know what you guys are talking about. It sounds to me as though we may have to go through all of this again."

Moynihan took a deep breath. "It's worse than that. We may be in the Court of Appeals and in the Supreme Court before we even get back to a trial—if a new trial is granted."

Lake heard Moynihan and slouched in his chair, dejected. But Martha Smith was in no such mood. "We will fight this thing to the bitter end. I know Arthur Lake didn't intend to kill Hannah and I know I didn't. Some place, some time, the truth will come out."

Martha's words hit me. Suddenly a thought occurred to me. "You know," I began, "as we look at the claim made by Traver, he really has opened a door for us. He is making a big deal about circumstantial evidence. Well, I think we may have a lot of circumstantial evidence he has not considered." I said to Moynihan, "You were not permitted to put into evidence, the story of Martha Smith, the story about how she and Arthur loved Hannah. I am sure there is a lot of information which was not put into the first trial but which we may put in now that Traver wants to emphasize circumstantial evidence. I think that with work we can demonstrate that Lake's motives were not something to sustain a verdict of murder, but would prove Lake's innocence."

Moynihan heard me out. "That's a huge chore, Mark, and I'm not sure we can produce enough new evidence. Right now I'm planning an argument against Traver's motion for a new trial on the basis of your argument that a new trial would constitute double jeopardy."

There was no longer any doubt in my mind that my so-called sub-plot might have a great deal to do with the question of whether Arthur Lake had killed his wife—thanks to Mr. Traver. Every little circumstance had to be explored to find the truth. If circumstance was to be determinative, we must put into evidence of story of the lives of Arthur Lake and Martha Smith.

The trial court denied the prosecution's motion for a new trial. In essence it accepted Moynihan's argument.

Travis appealed the trial court's decision. It was inconceivable to me as well as Moynihan that the court of appeals would overrule the trial court.

9

I went back to Breckenridge to learn more about Martha Toller and Jimmy Smith. Jimmy was an icon and everybody had something to say about him. Martha, however, was another story. There were only three retired teachers who could tell me anything about her.

At the high school, the principal gave me the address and telephone number of Mrs. Maria Garcia, who had taught Martha and Jimmy during the fifties. When I called Mrs. Garcia, I told her I was doing research on Jimmy Smith and Martha Toller.

"Oh my," she laughed, "you want to know about the 'odd couple'? I don't know that I can help you." She went on, "But I can tell you that I remember those people very well, and I'll be glad to talk to you." She gave me directions to her clapboard house on a tree-lined street that saw very little traffic. I had no trouble getting there.

I found Mrs. Garcia an amiable, intelligent lady of sixty. Her brown hair had a few silver streaks in it. I told her I was surprised when she had referred to Jimmy Smith and Martha Toller as the "odd couple."

"Well," she explained, "Jimmy Smith was thought to be the handsomest man in the country. Martha weighed more than one hundred seventy-five pounds, though she was taller than average, perhaps five-foot-nine inches. Her face was plain, and her hair was never fixed or permed. She never paid any mind to appearances. She was a brainy one, though, with an IQ of one hundred sixty, and most likely had no time for trivial things like hairdos or fancy dresses. But she and Jimmy were inseparable. They had been friends since eighth grade. That's pretty young to be so close."

"You know them well, it seems."

"We had a unique system in school, very advanced for the time. At other schools teachers served as counselors as part of their regular duties, but I was the ombudsman for the entire senior class. That was my only job. Ordinarily, an ombudsman is one who investigates complaints of individuals, but I did more than that. I actually got into the lives of the students. I interviewed them when they were juniors and not only got to know their academic records but also their homes, their parents, even their relatives in order to help them focus on their future. I kept a complete record on each student.

"As an eighth grader, Jimmy Smith was a handsome child and a fair student. He had many friends. Even in the eighth grade he was the star athlete. He played football, basketball, and baseball, both in and out of school. He had no other interests. The older he got, the more muscular and the handsomer he got. The girls adored him, not only because he was good looking but because of his modest, quiet demeanor.

"Martha was not one to attract boys or men, because she was just plain homely and because she made no effort to make herself attractive. She was totally absorbed in Jimmy Smith. For some reason, she didn't think it necessary to make herself attractive to him. That's why they were called the 'odd couple.'

"What Martha had among her peers was respect. She was forever providing answers to fellow students' problems. She did this in a kindly way, not as a superior student looking down at people not so gifted as she. She was unassuming. She never made a fellow student feel stupid. That's why, in her own way, she was as adored as Jimmy.

"Martha was valedictorian of her class. Mr. Nicker, the

principal had her in an American History class. In two weeks, she read and outlined the textbook. Mr. Nicker had to ask her not to come to class because she so dominated it. She got her 'A' anyway. She organized the first and only student newspaper. She was editor and she also was financial officer. She sold ads to the local merchants who were glad to help her."

"What drew them together?" I wondered.

"That's a tough question," Mrs. Garcia replied. "Nobody knows what ties bind people or why the bind endures. My guess is that Martha, in her own inimitable fashion, decided this handsome, pleasant young man would be her man. As for Jimmy, he was puzzled by life generally. Despite being popular, he felt inadequate, not only in his studies, but in dealing with people away from the gridiron. His abilities were natural. He never considered himself better than anybody else and the adulation of others left him confused. As many have observed, he never 'let his popularity go to his head.' He never appreciated that he was something special. This state of mind led to his friendship with Martha. With her he felt secure. He could ask her anything. She could handle all of his problems. She was his 'safety blanket.' And as the years passed and the pressure grew on Jimmy, he got closer to Martha, principally as a refuge, but also as a very grateful companion."

"What were their home lives like?"

"Jimmy lived with his grandmother, Bessie Smith. He never knew his father. He rarely saw his mother; she lived and worked in Detroit. Sarah would call her mother, Jimmy's grandmother, but never asked to talk to him. Rarely did she help financially. His grandmother managed the local laundromat. With her meager earnings she tried to feed and clothe herself and her grandson.

"Martha was the daughter of Marvin and Ida Toller. They both worked and maintained a modest home for Martha. She was an only child, as was Jimmy."

I was grateful for the opportunity to talk to someone who had known Martha Toller and Jimmy Smith well. It was more than I had expected. "Since it was your job to evaluate students and perhaps help them prepare for the future, what can you tell me about these two people from that perspective?"

"That's an interesting question. Interesting because it touches upon the most bizarre aspect of their lives. Jimmy was an athlete and only an athlete, albeit the best ever to attend Breckenridge. He was urged to go to college but although he would have liked that very much, he, felt he had to go to work immediately to help his grandmother. Martha was considered a student who should not only go to college but to graduate school. When I talked to Martha about her future she told me that her future was with Jimmy and she would not go to college if that meant she was to be separated from him.

"Ordinarily I would consider such an attitude juvenile, but Martha was no average teenager. She was mature beyond her years. I said to her, 'Martha, you owe it to yourself and to your parents to make the most of yourself.'

"To my astonishment she replied, 'I know that Jimmy has all the qualities to make a great future for both of us. With his athletic ability and his looks, he can be a national figure. With or without a Ph.D. I would be just another teacher. I think that with a little planning we can achieve a lot more together than we can separately.'

"This seventeen-year-old then proceeded to tell me that Jimmy was good enough to play in any big university and then in professional football. She would help him all the way. They would marry, have a family and live happily—and that's all she wanted."

"How did Jimmy respond to this program?"

"I asked her that, and she said, 'I haven't talked to him about it yet. I know I must do that soon. I'm sure it will take a lot of persuading on my part. Jimmy has no idea what his potential is.'

"There was nothing I could do to change her plans. She'd thought everything out for herself and for Jimmy as well. I did ask how she proposed to realize her plans, and her response was brief and to the point: 'Jimmy will get a football scholarship and I will get a job and the two of us will get him through college.' She even knew what kind of job she'd get. 'I'll work in a bookstore,' she said, 'and I'll go to night school and get certified as a tax-preparer and maybe a real estate agent.' "

I knew that Jimmy went to the University of Michigan and from there to the National Football League and the movies, but what happened to Martha? "Where did her plans go awry?" I asked.

"I'm not sure," Mrs. Garcia said. "I can't even tell you how Jimmy got into college. I had nothing to do with it. Del Martin, the football coach, helped with that. As for Martha, we sent her transcripts to Michigan as she later requested, but I don't know if she attended or what happened to her after that."

When I showed her the picture of Martha Smith, she said, "I've seen that picture before and I've read about Jimmy Smith, the movie star as well as about Michelle Morgan. I know nothing about that. I can tell you that this picture is not a picture of the Martha Smith I knew as a high-school girl."

There was no point in pressing the point with Mrs. Garcia. I asked her how I could reach Mr. Del Martin and she directed me to the office of the superintendent of schools.

Del Martin had retired to Florida. A current phone number was on record, and I was able to learn from him how Jimmy Smith got into Michigan. It turned out that Jimmy himself had almost nothing to do with it. Martha had arranged it all! First, she managed to convince Jimmy he would be able to help his grandmother much better if he got a college education. "Then she persuaded me to tell Jimmy he was good enough for college and professional football," Mr. Martin told me. "I asked Martha why Jimmy wasn't speaking for himself. You see, I'd already talked to Jimmy and he told me he had to get a job to help his grandmother. 'Are you Jimmy's manager?' I asked her. She told me Jimmy was just too shy to push himself, so she was doing it. The boy had talent I'd never seen before, so I told Martha to get him over to the gym the next day. I had him run the forty yard dash; he did it in four-point-five seconds. He weighed two hundred thirty pounds and stood six feet three inches. I sent those statistics and a letter of recommendation with a summary of Jimmy's performance in the past two years. I told the Michigan backfield coach that Jimmy had been chosen All-Conference both years, breaking records for yardage gained as well as for number of tackles on defense. As with many high-school players in those days Jimmy played both ways. In thirteen out of the sixteen games he played in two years, he'd played sixty minutes.

"Meanwhile, Martha talked to Jimmy in that quiet but forceful manner she had, explaining why all of this was being done. She assuaged his sense of duty to his grandmother by assuring him that he could provide much better for her if he were a college graduate."

It was clear that Martha Toller and Martha Smith were the same person. They had the same initiative, drive and determination. Moreover, they had the same name and were born in the same town. At some point, Martha Toller Smith had taken charge of herself the way she took charge of her husband, but whereas Jimmy Smith was well-known his wife had ceased to exist, so far as Breckenridge was concerned. Mrs. Garcia could guide me only to the University of Michigan where Martha's transcripts had been sent. She did not know whether Martha had actually attended the school or what had become of her.

Breckenridge had lost track of her; she wasn't important enough to be maintained on the school's records. Everybody knew where the football star and movie idol was. No one knew about or cared about the woman he'd married. An even greater mystery surrounded their children, if indeed they were the children of both Martha and Jim. I knew the twins existed, for I had met them and was falling in love with one of them, but I could find no birth records in Ithaca or Ann Arbor or in the state record of births.

10

I called Roxanne on Sunday and she promptly hung up on me. I tried again with the same result. I couldn't blame her. I'd been rude and thoughtless. Truth to tell, I didn't want to go out with Roxanne. It wasn't fair to pretend otherwise. I decided to write a gentle letter exculpating Roxanne. *Mea culpa,* I would write, I'm in love with Michelle Morgan. But was that true? I decided not to write until I knew who I was. And that, I realized ruefully, might take years.

Meanwhile, I started to piece together the story of Jimmy and Martha at the University of Michigan from interviews with Ted and Margie Strange, and others, plus a bit of detective work that would have pleased Edward G. Robinson in *Double Indemnity.*

I learned that Jimmy was admitted to Michigan on a football scholarship which provided a dormitory room and two meals a day. They arrived on campus in late July. Jimmy reported to the gymnasium every day at 3 P.M. to lift weights, handle other muscle-developing machinery, and jog around the track. Michigan boasted an excellent academic program, and its football program, which was always at the top of the national rankings.

Martha rented a room in a house in Ann Arbor owned by Ted and Margie Strange and soon found a job at a local bookstore. She worked from 9 A.M. to 5 P.M. four days a week. Jimmy had duties at the dormitory in the morning and attended an afternoon drama class. This had come as a surprise to Martha, who asked the coach about it. She was told that it benefited both the university and the student athlete. Training in drama and speech enabled the athlete to maintain composure under pressure from the media and made the university look good as well. Moreover, the university might want him to participate in certain projects involving children, hospitals, and charities. It was necessary that he have a certain poise, to say nothing of what it would do for Jimmy in life after football.

Martha saw the value in this and encouraged Jimmy to audition for plays, helping him to memorize lines. She was counting on Jimmy becoming a "somebody" some day. He was the handsomest guy around and she was his manager.

That summer they got well acquainted with Ted Strange, a teaching fellow working on his Ph.D., and his wife Margie, who worked in the university counseling office. Together, they went on picnics in the park adjoining the university and to concerts, if tickets did not cost too much. And, of course, there were movies.

Martha talked to Margie about getting a Ph.D. Was it difficult? Margie said, "Not at all. Ted gets paid for teaching; I work in the personnel office; and by renting out a room we can afford to own a house in this beautiful town."

"How long have you been here?" Martha asked.

"A long time. We graduated from college together, and Ted is in his sixth year in graduate school."

"Six years!" Martha exclaimed. "How long does it take to get a Ph.D.?"

Margie laughed. "As long as we want," she answered. "There's no hurry. In fact, in order to get a Ph.D. in three or four years after undergraduate school, you've got to be independently wealthy, which we're not. If you don't have money it can take a long time, but we don't mind. My parents are well-off. They'd be glad to advance us the money, but Ted refuses to borrow it. Anyway, it's a lot of fun this way."

That's not for me, Martha thought. Why, in four years Jimmy would be playing football professionally, God knew where, and she would still be trying for her Ph.D. No way!

The last two weeks of August were tough. Jimmy had football practice twice a day, at 9 A.M. and 3 P.M. He could eat at the athletic dormitory or they could eat out together, but they could not afford to eat out very often. More often than not, he would go to the dorm and she would get a sandwich someplace. By the beginning of September Jimmy was truly a physical specimen. They weighed and measured him and took his photo for the official football program, which was passed out at the games. Jimmy was six feet three inches tall and weighed two hundred thirty pounds. He was the best looking player on the field and his figure was perfect. Ted and Margie kept the program as a keepsake, and showed me a scrapbook filled with Jimmy's exploits on and off the field.

The Stranges became their closest friends. Martha could relate to Margie. Her counseling position involved interviewing students with problems, academic or otherwise, and Martha learned a lot from her. Among other things, she learned that it would be best if she and Jimmy got married as soon as possible.

As they sat on a bench grilling steaks one day, Margie said "You two should be married and living together. Jimmy doesn't have to live in that dormitory. You make enough money to cover the extra cost." Then Margie gave her the punchline. "There are lots of rich, good-looking gals around here. It's going to be tough holding on to him. Every woman will want him."

This had occurred to Martha, but she said to Margie, "We plan to marry, but we aren't ready yet."

Margie smiled. "Do you expect to stay single until you both graduate? Let me tell you something, you can't hold onto him that long. Your guy is just too good a hunk. Once his name is in all the papers—and it will be—he'll be gone. Mark my words."

Margie's remarks became prophetic as soon as Jimmy's name made the headlines and his picture began appearing in the papers. Few people knew of her relation to Jimmy, and everywhere she heard women exclaim about him. Some even said they would like to spend the night in bed with him. This was another world to Martha. She was silent while they talked about him in a pornographic way until she could stand it no longer and had to leave. She knew enough not to tell them that Jimmy Smith was her fiancé. She came to understand that Jimmy Smith belonged to every woman—not just to her."

Just before the opening home game in which Jimmy played for only five minutes, carrying the ball twice for an unspectacular total of eight yards, Martha decided to press for marriage.

On the Sunday after that first game, Jimmy told her that Bill Mayes, an assistant coach, had taken him aside and told him he might be starting in the backfield before the season ended. Mayes said he would be willing to review films with him on Sunday and teach him how to read the field. Mayes wanted to meet with him between eight and nine each Sunday morning. When Jimmy told Martha about this, she was as excited as he was, thought it put an end to their Sunday picnics.

Jimmy met with coach Mayes as scheduled each Sunday and he worked hard because he loved football and because he always listened to Martha. Martha suggested he major in communications. It would help his career if he prepared himself for something more than coaching when his athletic skills declined. Jimmy took the required courses as well. He was getting the best education possible to fit in Martha's dreams.

In the last two games of the season, Jimmy came into his own. He was using his speed and his strength to break tackles and gain yardage. Moreover, he learned how to block, something he had not done in high school. Again, Margie Strange was the source of this phase of Jimmy's and Martha's lives.

The news stories I found in Ted and Margie's archives sang his praises. His picture in full football regalia appeared everywhere. He had a fan club before he'd earned a starting position. Magazines and newspapers heralded his integrity as well as his good looks. People noticed him and by his second year were asking him for his autograph on the street and in stores.

From the Stranges I learned that Martha continued tutoring him, and he managed to pass most of his courses. When it came to football, however, he was an excellent student. It came naturally to him, and he loved the game. As a sophomore his name was becoming a household word on campus.

He handled reporters with ease and charm, thanks to his courses in communication. He had more confidence in himself, and he was changing in other ways as well. No longer shy, he enjoyed the attention he was getting.

The university asked Jimmy to go to university-sponsored events at children's hospitals. There he was photographed with some of the women staff members as well as infirm kids. It was all heady stuff, but Jimmy was essentially the country boy from the sticks. It was part of his charm.

Martha made sure Jimmy kept in touch with his grandma by phone. She was pleased that he was making something of himself. And Martha's parents were proud of them, too. Jim's mother, Sarah Smith, was another story. After years of not hearing from her, he started getting letters. He gave the very first letter he got from her to Martha, and she showed it to the Stranges, who reported it to me. "I'm so proud of you," the letter read. "I'd like to see a game." Martha wondered if Jimmy would recognize her. He told her, "It's been seven years since I last saw her." The Stranges were shocked when they heard Jimmy say this. They repeated his words to me.

Martha got tickets for his grandmother and his mother when Michigan played its next game. His grandmother welcomed the chance to see Jimmy, in or out of football uniform, but his mother was thrilled to sit in the crowd, watch him play, and inform everyone around them that Jimmy Smith was her son when he scored the winning touchdown.

They took Jimmy's mother and grandmother to a restaurant after the game, and afterwards waved good-bye as the women drove back to Breckenridge, two hundred miles away. Now Martha told Jimmy it was time they got married and rented an apartment so they could entertain friends and family at home The few times previous that they had talked about it he had been quiet. According to Ted, he was no longer gung ho to get married. Not that he refused. He just wanted to put it off.

"Remember," he said, "we talked about completing college first."

Martha told Margie that they had planned to get married while still in school, if it were at all possible, but she didn't remind him of that discussion. She used a more positive argument instead.

"It will be so much nicer to have our own apartment," she argued. "Look at how we'd have to treat your mother and grandmother. We have no place to be alone with them. And there will be others. For example, we have been in the Stranges' house. We should have them as our guest; it's only fair."

He said nothing, but after the next game, he proposed. They got married a week later, Ted and Margie the only witnesses, and rented an apartment. It was a simple civil ceremony.

Jimmy's encounter with his mother apparently had been a non-event. There was no fond embrace, no tears of joy. Martha felt sorry for Jimmy. How does one greet a mother one has never known and from whom one has had neither love nor affection? It was an awkward situation. Martha had tried to be gracious with Jimmy's grandmother and mother, but they remained cold and reserved. Martha accepted this in silence. She was sad about it, but she was not about to start a feud.

11

The events which occurred after the first game following their marriage were foreboding. I got the story from Margie and Ted, whom Martha had invited to dinner. Jimmy did not start but got into the game toward the end of the first quarter. He ran three plays and left the game. Michigan punted and the half ended with Minnesota ahead by a score of 21–0.

It was unusually cold and the crowd was sullen. In the second half, Jimmy ran wild. He had three long runs of at least twenty yards, caught two passes and was the player of the game. Michigan won 35–28. As they left the stadium, Jimmy's name was on everybody's lips. Martha was delighted. Her dream was coming true.

When they reached their apartment, Martha went into the kitchen to finish the meal she had started, and Jimmy went into the bedroom. Soon he came out wearing his best suit. Martha was surprised. "I've got to go to the Student Affairs Building," he said.

Martha remonstrated. Dinner would soon be ready and they were expecting guests. "I've got to go to this affair," Jimmy replied. "The alumni association is sponsoring a get-together and a dinner. My presence is required."

"You never said anything to me about such a meeting," Martha exclaimed.

"Sorry, I forgot," he said. "Ted and Margie will understand. I've got so many things to do now that I forget some things." He opened the door and was gone. She didn't get a chance to ask him if wives were invited.

Martha stayed up until 11 o'clock waiting for him. She wanted to talk to him about the day, about how rude he'd been to Margie and Ted. At 11 o'clock she went to bed. At 3 A.M. she found him sleeping on the couch in the living room, fully clothed. She left orange juice, cereal, toast, and coffee for him and went to work. Although it was Sunday, she had started doing the books for the bookstore and this was the only day she had free to work on them.

The Stranges told me about this occasion when they had had dinner with Martha without Jimmy. They also recounted to me what Martha had told them about the events following that unhappy meal as related to them by Martha.

As she drove to the store that morning she wondered how he could be so inconsiderate. She knew that Jimmy was now a celebrity of sorts and that as he became more famous she would see less of him. She vowed not to become a nagging wife. At the same time, Jimmy himself was changing. In discussions with her, he had started to assert himself. She concluded that this was probably true of all marriages. If so, she could handle it!

She returned from work at noon. Jim was not there. Pushing anxiety aside, she started the Sunday meal. She was placing the meal on the table when he walked in. She forced a big smile and asked him if he was ready for Sunday dinner. She was determined not to complain. Jim's expression was serious as he said, "Let's sit down. Let's talk for a minute." Martha put down the plates, came to the chair where he was sitting, stood behind him, and rubbed his shoulders. Without raising his head, he said, "I've been thinking. I'm sorry about yesterday. I didn't know how to handle the situation. I don't know why I didn't tell you about the dinner reception after the game. I was in a spot. I did what I had to do."

It was a good thing he wasn't looking at her. She couldn't contain her glee. She had feared something far worse. "I understand," she said. "The pressures are building up on you. We'll manage them."

"I feel bad about standing up Margie and Ted." That was as much remorse as she had ever seen in him. She told him they would understand; after all, they were friends.

When they sat down to breakfast the next morning he said in a quiet but determined way, "I don't like all of this banquet business."

She said calmly, "We don't live in Breckenridge anymore. This is a new world and you are a big part of it. We must adjust to it. We wouldn't be happy in our old world anymore. We must adapt. I will try if you will try." He got to his feet, came around the table, picked her up, and held her for a moment. He didn't say another word.

And yet, she wasn't sure where they stood. He was giving her a mixed message, but he still seemed to love her. That would have to be enough for the time being, she told Margie.

Ted and Margie still lived in the same house when I interviewed them. He was a tenured professor now and quite busy. I was only able to spend half an hour with him in his crowded office on campus, but Margie had plenty of time to reminisce. It was inconceivable to her that Martha had anything to do with Hannah Lake's murder.

"Martha was our last tenant," she said. "I became pregnant soon after Martha and Jimmy married, so we turned her room into a nursery. Come, I'll show it to you." She led me upstairs to a room decorated with movie posters. "Ted Junior is a civil engineer," she told me. "He lives in Phoenix, but I keep his room the way he left it. He and his wife, Julia, visit us once a year, alternating Thanksgiving and Christmas with visits to her folks in St. Louis." She said it in a wistful way, not to complain, but she clearly longed for more frequent contact. "Of course, we're often on the phone to one another."

Margie was short and stocky but full of energy. "Let's have some tea," she said. "I'll show you Jimmy's clippings." As I leafed through album after album, Margie puttered about the kitchen, unable to sit still for very long. "I told Martha she could have all my scrapbooks, but she wasn't interested. I don't blame her, really. She did everything for Jimmy, and he did whatever he pleased."

There were several pictures of Martha, but in only one was she with her husband, and according to Margie that was a candid shot Ted had snapped at a picnic. In that picture, a heavyset woman I would not have recognized as Martha was smiling at a man, unmistakably Jimmy, in the process of devouring a hot dog while Margie stood before a grill ladened with smoking sausages.

Most of the photos were of Jimmy and his teammates, though there were quite a few of Jimmy in hospital settings with different women. "The university wanted to get media recognition of the projects it funded, and the media wanted beautiful women and football heroes, not dowdy housewives," Margie explained. "Martha understood that the university liked to arrange for an attractive woman to attend charity events with Jim, and if this upset her she never let on, not even to me. They used a woman on the university staff or on the staff of companies serving the university. They even used me once," Margie said, pointing to a group photo in front of the new wing of a hospital. "They must have been particularly hard up that day."

I said something complimentary, though the clip had yellowed to where it was hard to distinguish the people in the photo. Reading the captions, I noted that a woman named Jane Fairbanks frequently appeared.

A slick magazine photo showed Jimmy holding a child of four or five years old. Beside him was a strikingly attractive young lady. Jimmy was wagging a finger at the child in a vain attempt to get a smile out of him. Jim was smiling, though, and so was the lady with him. "Gridiron great Jimmy Smith and hostess Jane Fairbanks entertain stricken youngster," read the caption. "Who's Jane Fairbanks?" I asked Margie.

"Bobbie Fisher's friend," Margie replied. "They worked for food services."

"Where can I find her?"

"I wouldn't know," Margie said. "Jimmy dated Jane for a while after he and Martha divorced, but I haven't seen her for twenty years now. Bobbie still works for food services. Maybe she knows."

I asked Margie if I might borrow the photo, tracked Bobbie Fisher down the following day, and showed her the photo. "I'm trying to locate the Jane Fairbanks," I said. "I understand you're her friend."

A slender, affable brunette, Bobbie looked at me quisically. "Who are you?" she asked.

I told her that I was trying to write the true story about Jimmy and Martha Smith. "Perhaps," I explained, "I'm trying to clear both of them of all the gossip which surrounds them."

"What's in this for you?" she shot back at me. I replied I'm interested in getting the record straight. I have no particular ax to grind."

"What makes you think Jane Fairbanks had any part in this so-called story about the Smiths?"

Again I explained "I have shown you photos of Jimmy and Jane Firestone. There are several of them. They seem quite attracted to each other."

Bobbie Fisher became angry. "That's the problem with you media people. You paint the picture, you construe the picture to create a problem."

I decided to become firm. "Was there a problem? I didn't say anything about a problem. I fully intend to get to the truth of the Lake murder case and one way or the other I'll learn what relation, if any, Jane Firestone had on the case."

"Well, I can tell you right now. She had absolutely nothing to do with that case. She did what she could to save Martha's marriage to Jimmy Smith."

I smiled. "So, she did have something to do about the marriage between Martha and Jimmy. I think Jane Fairbanks will greatly regret not having spoken out. The inferences, without an explanation from her, will not be favorable. And then you and she will claim I concocted some story about her and Jimmy Smith."

The only reason I could speak in this mode was that Ms. Fisher had indicated that Jane Firestone had somehow been instrumental in the breakup of the Jimmy/Martha marriage. The lady now saw this, saw what she had done. "I'll give you her phone number and you can get it straight from her."

When I got back to my office the next morning I found that Moynihan had called me. I returned his call. "Have you read the papers lately?" Moynihan asked. I told him I had been on the go and had not bothered to read the papers. "The diatribes have started again. I must talk to Martha and Arthur, but I'd like to talk to you first. Can you see me today?"

"I'll be right there if you have time," I replied.

My conference was short. First, he handed me a copy of the Sunday *State Journal.* On the lower right of the front page the headlines read: LAKE CASE APPEALED. The opening sentence read: "Prosecutor claims in the appeal that the jury deliberately ignored the alleged affair between the defendant and Martha Smith which, according to Prosecutor Traver, eliminated from the jury's deliberation, consideration of the motive of the defendant, the very heart of the prosecution's case." The rest of the article set forth the details of the relationship of the defendant and Smith, specifically quoting Martha's admission that indeed she and the defendant loved each other.

That seemed to me to be an accurate account of the matter. I said to Moynihan: "You certainly expected this, didn't you?"

"Yes, of course," was the response. "But all those wild people who thought them guilty are now shouting louder than ever," Moynihan continued. "I asked you to come over because

I wanted to discuss the appeal. I have already agreed to see Melinda and she may show up any time."

"What's really bothering me is that the Court of Appeals may agree with Traver. I'd say it's a fifty-fifty probability. This is an unusual case. I've never had anything like this before. What Traver may very well say to the court is: 'The jury treated this case as though the court should have taken it away from the jury and directed a verdict.' And he will ask the Court of Appeals if the trial record was such that they would have directed a verdict. He will point out that Lake was the only one who was present when the act of administering the extra morphine was committed; that there is no other explanation for the disappearance of the vial of morphine and though this was not enough to convict it may well have been had the jury considered the motives Lake had."

I repeated what I had said previously. It was enough that the jury had heard the testimony about the so-called affair and they could consider it or not, as they wished. It was not as though the testimony about the affair had been excluded from the record.

Moynihan hesitated. "I guess I have a concern that the judges have read all of the stuff appearing in the newspapers, radio, and television. They are human, too. And they must do nothing that will condone adultery—especially when the wife is an invalid."

At that moment Melinda Trudeau was ushered in by the secretary. Indeed she was Michelle's twin—same height, same hair, same general features. They were not identical but their resemblance was striking. Neither Moynihan nor I had met her before. She introduced herself to both of us. Moynihan asked her to be seated. He asked her: "What can I do for you? I assume you are here on *the* case and that is why I have not asked Mr. Pierce to leave. If you have some other matter Mr. Pierce will excuse himself."

"He is welcome to stay," Melinda replied. "I simply could not stay away and watch this thing by means of newspapers and radio and television. The people involved are my family. I've already been to California and talked to my father."

"My problem is that I know my mother and I know Uncle Arthur. And I also knew Hannah Lake. As I have thought about it I can see that nobody but those of us involved can understand. And that's what worries me. Our mother, Arthur Lake, Hannah Lake, and Rachel Strong and Michelle and I were a family! Hannah Lake really made us a family and we all adored her, including my mother and Uncle Arthur. Believe me, Hannah Lake was somebody whom you could not help loving. Our childhood was made beautiful by Hannah, Arthur, and Rachel. Sure my mother loved Arthur Lake. And she loved Hannah, too. And dear Rachel, our nanny. She saw it all. She can tell you and the court what our family was about.

"The stuff I read and hear makes me sick. The world is sick when it makes cheats out of my mother and Uncle Arthur. Can't anybody believe that Mother and Arthur Lake were always faithful to Hannah? Does that sound so preposterous?"

Melinda was near tears as she spoke. Moynihan, after allowing Melinda to compose herself, spoke in a soft voice, "Melinda, we are doing all we can to make the world and the courts understand. We all know that your mother and Arthur loved each other and they also loved, respected, and were faithful to Hannah. It's unfortunate that one reporter sees it as something you know is untrue. Mark Pierce here is trying to get the information which we need to show the truth. If there is a new trial we hope to be able to show what your family was. We'd like you and Michelle to testify."

At this point I asked Melinda: "Do you want to tell us of your meeting with your father?"

Melinda hunched her shoulders as though she was about to tell us something awful. She looked aside as she said: "That was the most bizarre experience of my life. At twenty-two years of age I learn that the great Jimmy Smith is my father! I really didn't want to see him! I forced myself to do it. I was not going through life saying I had refused to meet my father. I simply said to him in the living room of his apartment: 'I'd like to meet my father.' He said: 'And I'd like to meet the daughter I never knew I had!' And then we talked like a couple of strangers meeting for the first time. It was awful. What could I say? What could he say? He tried to help. He said: 'I'm so sorry it has to be like this. I'll take my share of the blame for this mess. If I had known we would have been much closer over the years. But I'm not blaming your mother. She has made a good life for you—better than I could. As she did with me, she did it all with you. That's your mother. There is one more thing—your mother is the one person who truly loved me.'

"I found out my father is a nice guy. I had thought I would meet a big, egotistical, self-centered guy. He isn't. Then, he said something strange. He said: 'I know I have no place in your family. Martha is your father as well as your mother. Believe me, I know Martha. But I'd like to look through the window now and then and see how you are doing.' I told him I was happy to know him and that he would always be a part of me. It got to be an emotional moment."

Then Melinda spoke to me. "You and Michelle pulled a fast one in California. That stopped one scandal. I see you are spending some time out there. How are you going to manage the engagement?"

"I don't have any problem with that. Michelle may have a problem. I'm ready to play my role as fiancé as long as I can."

"I remember you from high school," Melinda continued. She laughed. "Your story is at least a happy one. When my husband and I met her in Chicago last week, she said she enjoys being with you. She claims you are real—not a flake like so many people around Hollywood."

I returned her laugh with one of my own. "I guess all of us are still small-town folks."

Melinda was not finished. "You tell me that you will get all of the facts about our family and try to describe it to the jury. What worries me is that all that I know about our family is wonderful to me, but it could very well have the opposite effect on others. People prefer to see the worst side of everything. I'm afraid the more we tell the worse it will be. In Chicago Michelle told me she feels the same. She would rather this whole mess be permitted to die out."

"I'm afraid that isn't possible anymore," Moynihan advised. "We are back in court and we are trying to stay out of court without a trial. A trial will rehash all of the bad stuff and we will add something which we think is good but the jury may see it differently."

I added: "I'm going to go over this case with a fine-toothed comb. We want to present all of the story."

As soon as I had spoken Moynihan put in a sobering thought. The problem will be to get the story into evidence. We are hoping that since the prosecution wants to show motive by circumstantial evidence we can try to show the motive was not to harm the victim in any way."

12

I called Jane Fairbanks. Bobbie had given me both the residence and the business numbers. It was already nine o'clock Michigan time and therefore six o'clock California time. I called her home. Her answer was perfunctory, "Jane Fairbanks here."

"I'm Mark Pierce of Lansing, Michigan. I'm investigating the Lake murder case. I would like to ask you a few questions about Jimmy Smith. As you know he is the divorced husband of Martha Smith, a principal in the case."

"Yes," the lady responded in a firm, almost baritone, voice. "I've just read about Jimmy and his affair with his daughter, Michelle Morgan. I know Jimmy Smith and I had read about his running around with Michelle Morgan but this recent story about blew my mind. I know absolutely nothing about that or about Jimmy and Martha's marriage. I'm sure Jimmy had nothing to do with any murder."

"Why do you say that?" I asked.

"Because Jimmy Smith wouldn't kill a fly."

"Well, then you must have known him pretty well," I observed. "Bobbie Fisher told me that once you saved Jimmy's marriage. What was that about? Still, Jimmy eventually divorced Martha and he has learned only now that he has twin daughters, including Michelle Morgan. You must realize that this whole scene raises questions, which, if not answered, will be enlarged and scandalized with rumors."

"I don't follow your logic," the voice on the telephone intoned. "It would seem that Michelle Morgan explained what the gig was about. But I have nothing to hide. I'm ready to talk to you anytime."

Jane Fairbanks was now a vice president of the food service company for which she had worked in Ann Arbor. The company still served at the university and she had to be there on business the next week and agreed to see me at the campus. There I met an attractive lady in her forties, with a modest hairdo and a dark jacket and pantsuit. Her smile displayed perfect, glistening teeth. She was no petite girl. She was nearly as tall as I am. We met at the company's offices at the Student Affairs building.

Jane Fairbanks opened the discussion. "I am here because I know something about stories written about people's private lives and I hate doing this. But if I should say to you 'I will tell you nothing' then it is fair game for you and others to speculate and to come up with guesses which will damage those you write about. I don't know Martha Smith. I do know Jimmy Smith personally and I will do whatever I can to save him more trouble."

This was a fair basis for my interview. "Have you remained in touch with Jimmy?" I asked.

"No. It is now more than twenty years since I was close to him but I have never tried to contact him and he doesn't even know that I am in Los Angeles, not too far from him."

"You say you were close to him," I started. "What do you mean?"

"I loved the guy!" The straight answer startled me. Before I could ask more questions she said, "And so did every woman who saw him and got a chance to know him."

"I understand," I continued, "that you and he posed for pictures at the request of the public relations people for the university. That would be a rather platonic affair which doesn't tell us much. I confess to you that those pictures meant more to me than a platonic relation." I smiled.

"I told you that I loved him. And it was not a love I shared with a million other people. He also loved me. Or so he told me."

"But at that time he was still married to Martha," I replied.

"Yes, and that is why my affair with Jimmy had to be ended and I ended it."

"Well," I pressed, "that's a beginning. Tell me the details."

She launched into her story. "We got well acquainted in those picture sessions. We often had coffee or lunch after working. I found out Jimmy Smith was really a nice guy and no lying, egotistical public figure. And he was always anxious to be with me. I grew to like him very much. One day he called me and asked if he might see me and talk to me. I was pleased to talk to him. We met in the room at the Student Affairs building which Bobbie Fisher and I shared. We were alone. He told me he would very much like to be with me alone from time to time. This shocked me. This appeared to be the kind of proposition I had received from many men in the past. I said to him 'You are a married man. How can you talk to me that way?'

"He lowered his head and said nothing for a moment. He looked like a child who had misbehaved and knew it. And he was a child! He didn't give me the usual line of men on the prowl. He told me he was indeed married and he did not want to hurt his wife. That was why he wanted a secret relationship.

"Of course that raised several questions in my mind. I was about to cross-examine him when he continued. 'I've got to find a hideout where I can get away from the pressure. She is the one who pressures me most. She plans my life. She is always promoting me and telling me what I must do. Then there is Walter Harman, the guy who is my advisor. He tells me what to do. On top of that the university public relations people like to lead me around by the hand. And the football coaches watch every move I make and are always after me because all this publicity stuff is getting to be too much and is affecting the whole football squad.' Like a little boy trying to break his mother's apron strings he told me I was the only person he could relax with and be himself."

She hesitated. I did not question her as she seemed to be trying to recollect. "This little speech by Jimmy Smith simply floored me. Here was this 'big man' on campus, this national figure, the most handsome man in the country—and he was not such a person at all! He was just a nice, decent small-town guy completely without an ego, who was having trouble coping with it all. I felt sorry for him. I confess that I was also very much attracted to him, much more so when I found out more about him.

"I asked him what he would like me to do. He said he would like to just see me and drink coffee or eat cake or do anything with just the two of us."

I was dumbfounded. What kind of a relationship was this? I managed to ask: "And what happened?" She told me that they agreed to meet in her and Bobbie's room whenever he wanted to get together. They did this once and then Bobbie suggested she would move out and get another apartment. It was not possible for her to stay away just 'from time to time' even if it was only for an afternoon.

"It was impossible to simply meet at three o'clock and sit and chat for two hours or more. It might have been different if we had been able to go out. We could not do this. And so pretty soon we got familiar and then we became intimate. Somehow he could do this. He still professed love for his wife but he wanted me too. It was not long before I was having serious problems. Whatever might have been his intentions or desires—and it looked as though he wanted to have his cake and eat it as well—there was no place for me in this picture. Whatever I had done in my youth—and I was still young—this was something which could only bring trouble. I had to bring it to an end. But this was easier said than done. Bobbie kept after me to get a commitment out of him. 'Take him while you can,' she said. 'If you don't take him somebody else will. His wife will never be able to keep him.' "

"Meanwhile, his wife kept managing him. She decided he should specialize in communications so he could have a career after football. Then she decided he should act and she got a part for him in a dream club play, telling the drama department that if they starred the famous football player they would fill the house and get national recognition. He followed her orders and came to me for 'relaxation' as he put it.

"Bobbie and I went to one of his performances. He played the lead and he did well enough to get good applause. After the play Bobbie and I went to a restaurant for a late dinner. Lo and behold, the whole cast from the play shows up. He, of course, stood out over all the others. She was with him. I could not stand it. Bobbie and I paid our bill and left and she went to the apartment with me and watched me throw myself on the bed and pound my fist. I was crying. 'Quit playing games,' she said, 'take him while you can.'

"I thought about giving him an ultimatum. And then I thought, what if he decided to divorce his wife and marry me. Would I then be his manager, his director in everything he did? I doubted that he could do for himself what Martha was doing and I couldn't do it either. I decided to stop it all. I asked my company to take me back to headquarters in Los Angeles and I've been here ever since. I even got married. It didn't work. I'm afraid I was not a very good wife. So, here I am and you know my story."

Indeed this was quite a story. It sounded authentic. I still had questions. "Have you seen Jimmy Smith at all since you left Ann Arbor, Michigan?"

She answered: "Not personally. But of course I have seen his picture in all of the newspapers and on television. All of that was a natural consequence of his program in college. We have not spoken since Ann Arbor. I don't think he knows where I am or what I am doing. I never told him where I was going. It's been almost twenty-three years. It was not until Michelle Morgan made her disclosure that I learned that he was the father of twin daughters and that the Martha Smith in the Lake case is the Martha Smith who had been his wife in Ann Arbor. All these years I've followed Jimmy Smith's career and his affairs as the national lothario. But of his private life and that of the Martha in Ann Arbor I know nothing."

Jane Fairbanks continued, "Knowing what I have read of the Lake case I can now see that the Martha Smith running Jimmy Smith's life could very well be the same dynamo in business."

I left the meeting with Jane Fairbanks with a deep sense of frustration. Why this interview with this person? What had I learned? How will the information I got from this lady help me in my investigation? The question bugged me as I drove home. I finally decided that it was merely a matter of curiosity. Regardless of my original objectives, I simply had to know more about these characters! What had made them what they were? Slowly it was dawning on me that curiosity was what was driving public opinion. One must assuage the public's curiosity—one way or the other, whether guilty or innocent. "There is a difference" I said to myself, "between satisfying the demands of the law and the demands of curiosity. There are limits to the pursuit of justice. There are no limits in the pursuit of curiosity. However, as matters now stood these personal details might be a part of 'circumstantial evidence.' "

Jane Fairbanks' statement was at least a partial answer to this curiosity. One could not conclude what Fairbanks' story meant without further investigation. The Fairbanks statement confirmed my appraisal of Jimmy Smith. Second and third hand, it confirmed my estimation of Martha Smith. But Fairbanks did not know Martha Smith except through what Jimmy Smith had told her. Was there more to Martha Smith than I had gathered from Fairbanks and the prior interviews? I surprised myself by admitting that I was not so much interested in sustaining or condemning the verdict, as I was in learning about all of the people in this drama. And so was the public!

Condemning the verdict was merely a matter of expressing this frustration in not obtaining all of the little details in the lives of Jimmy, Martha, and Arthur and Hannah Lake. So, I convinced myself that it was worthwhile to learn all I could about each of these people. With the appeal this was really more than satisfying one's curiosity. It was the story which I hoped would persuade a new jury that there was no evil among these people.

13

I had dinner with the Stranges on Thursday and told them about my conversation with Jane Fairbanks.

"If Jane thinks Martha didn't know about her, or about the women who followed, she's mistaken. I became very close with Martha when she started having problems with Jimmy. She came to me just to have someone to talk to," Margie stated.

"What about the problems?" I asked.

"As Jimmy's fame grew and as he gathered more fans, particularly women, he became more independent and resentful of Martha's directives and machinations. He matured. He was now a big star. On the outside, he was the same laid back hick from Breckenridge, but he had a short fuse with Martha. I warned her that this would happen," she went on. "Even if Martha was a beauty she would not be able to hold him. When she married him it was no different."

"Perhaps, if Martha had not been so domineering there might have been a chance for her," Margie continued. "I remember the time she bought some trousers for Jimmy. Jimmy said, 'How do you know I will like them?'

"Now, Martha had bought almost all of Jimmy's clothes. He never took the time to shop for himself. His explosion over this mundane purchase made it clear to Martha things had indeed changed. Martha replied that she had always done this and he had never before complained. Jim's next remark was the killer, Margie continued. He shouted back at her, 'You never bought anything for me. You bought it for your doll. Yes, I've just been your doll, just like the dolls you had when you were a child. You have never loved me. You've loved your doll.'

"Martha shot back, 'Okay, big shot,' she said, 'You buy your own clothes from now on. I'll do what I want to do for a change. I'll look after myself. You look after yourself.' Martha grew so angry that she got up from the table, threw her napkin down and stomped out of the room."

"What did Jimmy do?" I asked.

"He started staying away more than ever, sometimes until the wee hours of the morning. The intervals between his presence at home grew longer. One morning over the breakfast table he told Martha he wanted a divorce. Ironically, Martha was about to tell him she was pregnant."

"You knew she was pregnant?"

"Of course I did. Who else would she tell? Not Jimmy. With divorce threatened, he'd believe that she was trying to trap him. It would only make matters worse, she told me."

Here at last was the verification I'd been looking for. "And so they divorced as quietly as they'd married," I surmised.

"Not exactly. Two weeks after the blow Martha got from Jimmy, his agent called on her at the store where she worked and asked her to have lunch with him at a nearby restaurant," Margie went on. "I remember this vividly after all these years, because she was so upset when she recounted what he had to say. Harman told her that it was necessary to get more photos of Jimmy with attractive women. Pictures of him in a football uniform were not enough. He said, 'I want you to know this is strictly promotional, purely a business proposition.'

"Can you imagine? First Jimmy tells her he wants a divorce and then Harman practically tells her to hide in a closet. Martha wondered if Jimmy's demand and Harman's remarks were part of a program to free Jimmy before the divorce! 'They can't wait until the divorce is final!' she cried.

"I asked her how she'd responded to Harman. She said, 'I asked him where I fit in his program,' and he replied, "You are still his wife,' She said, 'I know I'm his wife. I asked you where do I fit?' and he said, 'We must play down the fact that Jimmy is married. He has become every woman's sweetheart.'

"Martha wasn't the type of woman to bend when the going got tough. She asked the real question. 'Would it be different if I was a model like the girls you want for your pictures?'

"And he told her," Margie said, shaking her head disapprovingly. "He was a master, I'll give him that! 'Martha,' he said, 'you know that in show business sex is always just beneath the surface. A picture taken with a spouse is like a picture of family, of children, of mundane living. Show business is based on romance, on mystery. You've worked too hard to deny Jimmy his big chance.'

"What irony! Here she was a pregnant wife and she was being told her husband could have no family. No children, no wife. She didn't tell Harman she was pregnant. It would pose a threat to his plans. In fact, she was terribly hurt, though her demeanor was calm. 'Mr. Harman,' she said, 'You have told me of your plans and the reason for them. You have not asked for my approval. Therefore, this conference is ended.' Without another word, she left the restaurant, fighting back tears, her head held high. It wasn't until she turned the corner that her tears flowed freely and she ran all the way to this very house to tell me what had happened."

As I later learned, Martha did not keep her pregnancy a secret. At the court hearing when the divorce was entered, after all the proofs had been taken and the lawyer for Jimmy and the lawyer for Martha had declared that there was no significant property to divide, that the parties had divided their personal effects, the judge turned to Martha who was still on the witness stand, under oath, and asked if she was pregnant. She answered

"I might be," much to the surprise of Jimmy and the two lawyers. The judge said to the attorneys, "Were you aware of this?" Both said this was the first time they had heard of this.

Jimmy's lawyer then assured the court that if a child was born within the customary term of childbirth, arrangements would be made by which Jimmy would provide for the child.

This explained the notation in the divorce decree about support for any child born of the marriage in the future.

As Martha left the court, Harman came up beside her and gave her an envelope. She found two thousands dollars in currency when she opened the envelope as she left the building.

Jimmy left the apartment. Martha stayed on and continued to work at the bookstore. They did not see each other after that day in court although both were in town. Jimmy continued his rise in popularity with great play on the football field and a well-planned program to get his picture into as many publications as possible, all under the guidance of Harman. "There had never been any mention of Martha before the divorce," Margie told me, "and there was none now."

Martha's troubles were far from over. She would soon deliver. She could not stay on where she was; a no-children policy was in effect. She refused to go back to Breckenridge. She was desperate. Again she turned to her best friend, Margie, who told her she must inform Jimmy as was agreed in court. Martha refused. "He has not contacted me to see how I was getting along, not once in almost eight months." He knew where she lived, where she worked. It was not that he was so busy. It was, she told Margie, that he had already forgotten about her, cast her aside like a used toy or piece of old equipment. He had no more use for her. He had gotten out of her all he needed, and more. "Any man," Martha had exclaimed, "who has any regard whatsoever for a woman he was once married to and the child he was about to get, would not turn his back on her and deliberately ignore her."

Martha refused to go back to Jimmy on 'bended knees,' and ask for help. She had always done things on her own and she would face this challenge as she had faced others: alone.

Margie arranged for Martha to go to her parents' home in Connecticut, which is where her twins were born. Mrs. Morris, Margie's mother, gave her the baby carriage in which Margie had ridden as an infant.

Where would she go from Connecticut? She could not go back to Ann Arbor or Breckenridge. She had to go someplace where she could make a lot more money than she had earned at the bookstore. She wrote Margie of her decision to follow the action. She would tackle New York City. Margie called her immediately and told her in no uncertain terms that she would be lost in New York. Manhattan was not the place for a single mother with two babies. Work would not be easy to get and she would not be able to rent an apartment she could afford. To all of this, Martha answered, "And where do you think I should go?"

"Back here," Margie retorted. "You can get your job back and a lot of people know you. You would be among friends. In New York you will be less than nothing."

"Jimmy is still there," Martha told Margie. "I won't live in the same town with him."

She informed her parents of the divorce and of the two daughters, and they said that she was welcome to return home, but Martha knew that would never do. Before leaving Connecticut, she tried to rent a New York apartment by telephone. Rent for what she wanted, she was told, started at fifteen hundred dollars per month. Moreover, most landlords wouldn't rent to a single mother with two infant daughters.

Undeterred, she took a plane, with her two girls and a baby carriage, and managed, through the Housing Commission, to get an apartment for three hundred fifty dollars a month in Queens. She would take the IRT to work each day like a million other New Yorkers.

14

From Rachel Strong I learned the rest of the story. Martha had more than fifteen hundred dollars left of the money Walter Harman had given her. She hoped that would last until she found a job. She bought clothes for her girls and flew to New York. That was a real chore, handling two infants in a crowded airport and on an airplane. She had never been so completely alone. Her girls were company but not the kind of company she needed. She needed a friend, or two, or three. She was absolutely alone. Her only touch with the world was the letters she wrote to her parents and to Margie Strange. The responses to those letters kept her alive.

Martha knew her parents would say, "She has ruined her life. There will be no more college education, no Ph.D. She will struggle to take care of her two daughters. Whatever their father provides will never be enough." At least her parents were good enough not to say, "We told you so." They never reminded her that she could have gone to college, gotten a Ph.D., but she knew what they were thinking: *This is what you get for the years of dedication to the success of the man you loved! How stupid to be so old-fashioned, to follow the tradition that a wife must dedicate her life to her husband and the family!*

Well, she did have a family, and she was grateful for that, and she would take care of her children without help from anyone!

If Jimmy Smith didn't care if she had children, if his agent didn't know, she wouldn't tell them, though both should have known and could have known if they had had enough interest to inquire.

For four long years, Martha made her way in New York. Most people would not dream of trying to live in New York City, but Martha Smith had great confidence in herself. If she was to make it big, she must do it in a big place, and New York offered the greatest opportunity, so she thought. It proved to be a most trying ordeal.

Martha had a duffel bag with all of her belongings in it and a little carriage, not much larger than a doll carriage with her two daughters in it. She tried dragging the duffel bag while pushing the carriage. Finally a porter came to her rescue and helped her down two flights of steel subway stairs.

As she approached the apartment building in which she had rented an apartment sight unseen, she could see that there were four buildings with basketball courts and broken swings in the middle of the complex. The apartment houses were old and the hallways spray-painted with graffiti. A teenager helped her find the right building and carried her duffel bag into the lobby. Martha's apartment was on the top floor, the eighth floor. When she reached the top floor she realized she had left her key to the apartment in her duffel bag in the lobby. Could she leave her children in the hall while she went down eight floors to get the key? She could not. It was too dangerous. She piled them back into the elevator, went downstairs and got her duffel bag. Then it was back to the elevator, up to the eighth floor.

She opened the door to what was to be her apartment and was shocked. The living room was filthy. There were paper, cigarette butts, and even toilet paper all over. She went into the kitchen. The sink was full of water, obviously plugged. The toilet was worse. She went into the bedroom. The bed was not just unmade, the sheets were filthy. The place was simply uninhabitable! She was now desperate. Of course the hall phone would not reach the office. The phone in the apartment was disconnected. She was now terrified. What was she to do? Where was she to go? As she pondered her predicament and as the two little girls began to stir, a woman came to the door.

"That woman was me," Rachel told me proudly. "I'd been watching Martha's comings and goings, and before she could object, I said to her, 'Come with me, bring the children. I'll carry the duffel bag.' They went across the hall to Rachel's apartment. Rachel then said to Martha, 'You stay here with me. It may be a little crowded, but we'll manage.'

Martha was in a state of shock. She could not even bring herself to thank the lady who now took Michelle out of the carriage and held her. "I want you and your children to sleep in my bed," she said. "I'll sleep on the couch. First, let's get the children fed and bathed and you sit down and relax."

At this point, Martha started to cry. With Michelle in one arm, Rachel went to Martha and put her other arm around her. "I'll call the office," she said. "It will take a few days to clean your apartment. The people who stayed there were not nice people. You will stay here while they clean your apartment."

Still in shock Martha managed to say, "How can I ever thank you?"

"You don't have to thank me, girl," Rachel replied as she moved the baby carriage toward the bedroom. "You lie down on the couch and compose yourself."

Rachel Strong had lost a husband and two sons to drugs. They were dead, but Rachel was a survivor and detected the same resilience and resourcefulness in her new neighbor.

Rachel asked Martha about herself, and Martha told her this was her first visit to New York. "Why come to New York? It's too hot in the summer, too cold in the winter, and everyone's mean and nasty."

Martha told her that she needed a job that paid well. "New York's the best place for that, I'm told."

"So, you don't have a job?"

"No, but I'm going to start looking for a job right away."

"And who's going to look after your children while you look for work."

"I'll get a babysitter," Martha said.

"Hmmm-mmm," Rachel said. "Have some fudge. It's from Memphis, same as me." Rachel knew that it would be difficult for Martha to find a job, but she did not want to discourage the young mother. She warned Martha, however, not to be surprised if it took longer than she thought.

"Why is that?"

"Well, what I hear is that every company in New York has a list of people they can hire if they need more help. They will add you to the list, but it may be some time before your name comes up."

Martha thanked Rachel for the advice but was confident she could get a good job. First, she must get a babysitter. "Don't try that," Rachel declared in a louder, sharper tone. "I'll take care of your children while you look for work." Martha thanked her and told her that her help was more than she could accept.

The very next morning Martha went out and bought the *New York Times* and turned to the Help Wanted section. Much to her surprise, she found herself eliminating most of the employment offers. She was not qualified for many jobs, and those she was qualified for she simply didn't care to do. There were jobs for welders, painters, nurses, nurses aides, and domestic services. Two ads for secretaries appealed to her, and she decided to try those. The first was with Barwick Fabric Co., a nationwide developer of synthetic fabrics for the clothing industry located on the Brooklyn waterfront.

It was a tough neighborhood, but she willed herself protected and no one accosted her. In a dingy office she encountered a man in his fifties with a balding head and thick glasses to whom she gave her name. "I'm here to apply for the job," she said. The man eyed her from head to toe. He was so deliberate about it that it seemed like minutes before he asked her to have a seat. She told him she was a graduate of a correspondence school and had kept accounts and handled correspondence. She also told him that she maintained records for inventory.

He asked her if she had a college background, and she said, "No." Next he asked her if she was a high school graduate, and she told him that she had been class valedictorian and had a 3.9 grade point average.

"How long have you lived in New York?"

"Two weeks."

"Where?"

"The Metropolitan Public Housing Complex in Flushing," she said, and he frowned.

"You married? Got kids?" She explained that she was divorced and had two daughters. "How old?" She told him they were four months old and that she had made arrangements for their care. "If you work here, will you move?" he wanted to know.

She told him she was willing to move and that her babysitter would go with her. She thought she was giving him the answers he wanted, but suddenly the man got to his feet and extended his hand. "I'm sorry," he said, "but we look for somebody with experience in a big company. So good talking to you. Good-bye." And that was the end of that employment interview.

As she walked through the reception area on her way out, she noticed that most of the women were thin, well-dressed, and quite sophisticated. She certainly was not in their league. These women were models. She could never be a model. She recalled how the man who interviewed her had looked her over before he asked a question.

When she got back to the apartment she said to Rachel. "I struck out."

Rachel tried to bolster her. "That's no disaster," she said. "Now we go to the next place. You must apply for welfare. Everybody in this building is on welfare. It's the only way you can make it."

"No," Martha said. "I have another job interview tomorrow." This company was the Braden Manufacturing Co. Martha didn't know what the company made, and that disturbed her somewhat. At the office, she was greeted by a lady who resembled the models she had seen in the previous office. Martha was asked the same basic questions and gave the same answers. The lady querying her was courteous, and at the end of the half-hour interview she told Martha that she would be advised when the decision on her employment would be made. She also told her that there were nine other applicants, two of whom had college degrees. A week later Martha received a letter thanking her for her interest and advising her that she had not gotten the job.

She went to several employment offices on East 42nd Street in Manhattan. She told them about her interviews and asked them if they could help her. She was told that the jobs they had available did not pay well. "When you factor in travel and the cost of sitters, you may find that you cannot afford to leave welfare and take a job with the firms we represent."

Martha explained she was not on welfare, and one lady suggested she get on welfare. "On welfare," the lady explained, "you will have Medicaid to help pay medical expenses and enough money to get by day-by-day. You may not do as well with one of our jobs."

When Martha returned to the apartment she found the girls asleep in a little bed just big enough for the two of them. When she asked how that got there, Rachel explained she had paid five dollars for it at a garage sale which she and the girls had attended. Martha thanked her and told her she would repay her.

Rachel became Melinda's and Michelle's aunt. More than that, Martha realized that she was a caring person whom she would come to love as she had Margie. At that moment, this black woman was her only source of solace, the only friend she had in the Big Apple.

Much as she disliked it, Martha applied for welfare and was accepted. Immediately she got a repaired refrigerator which was much better than the one that came with the apartment. But her troubles continued. If she took a job she would lose welfare. With welfare she was assured medical treatment for her babies. Without it she could not afford it. What was really getting to her was the fact that she could not get a job which paid enough to permit her to give up welfare. She could do some work and stay on welfare but that had a strange twist. The employer knew you were on welfare. He could tell you that he could not pay you more because that would cause you to lose welfare. She could not find a job which fit well with welfare and provide enough money to live a little better.

She wanted to buy some new suits for the girls but could not spare the money. Suddenly, the girls were dressed in those very suits. Rachel had spent part of her savings on them. This made Martha feel guilty, because she still had more than a thousand dollars of the money Harman had given her. That was for an emergency, she told herself, not for clothing.

15

Martha applied for jobs that were less demanding, but she could only find temporary work typing or filing. The jobs were never integral to a company's operation. She was learning nothing, and she was bored. The only thing she learned about working in an office was that a woman needed beauty far more than she needed brains! Were employers only interested in women as decorations?

Another hurdle she could not overcome was her lack of a college degree. This stopped her for a while. In the back of her mind was the haunting memory of how she had deliberately sacrificed a college education in order for her ex-husband to have one. The thought caused her considerable pain until she learned that her lack of college education masked the real reason she wasn't hired, namely that she did not have the body or face of a model. Other women lacked a college education and were able to find meaningful employment! Her pain was now tinged with anger. But what could she do? College was out of the question. And a college degree was no guarantee her physical flaws would be overlooked.

After our initial difficulties, Rachel Strong and I had become friends. Profanity and coarse language offended us both, and we both had a sweet tooth and a fondness for old movies. Besides, Martha had asked her to be as helpful as she could. "Who is Martha Smith?" I asked her "What is she?"

The angular African-American woman paused for a moment to gather her thoughts. Then she said, "I have been with this woman for nearly twenty-five years. I've witnessed her life, every nook and cranny, but I'm not sure I know who she is. There are people like that. One knows them and yet doesn't know them. One is never sure one has perceived every part of the life you seek to understand. I do know that she is not a split personality, that she is a well-balanced person. But I cannot predict what she may say or do next. I have concluded that the apparent split personality is the result of a brilliant mind housed in a not so attractive body and projecting mixed signals. For the most part, until recently, she didn't care how she looked. She once told me that 'looks shouldn't matter' and for her they don't. Martha's apparent split personality is due not so much to her actions but to the stereotype which all of us try to impose on people. I think I know something about stereotyping, I've lived with it all my life."

As I listened I concluded that I was talking with a highly intelligent, knowledgeable woman. If I had thought I was talking to a nanny, someone who looked after children and cleaned house, I would have been sorely mistaken—that was not who Rachel Strong was!

I was once again interviewing her in my law office, a week or so after my meeting with Jimmy and Martha, a meeting called to discuss Owen's soon to be released story concerning Arthur and Martha on the T.V. show *Inside Hollywood.* I'd bought a little time by promising Harriet a live exclusive and had practically lived on a plane since then. I had a plan and the approval of Martha and Arthur, but I had to know everything for my plan to work. There'd been too many surprises already; I didn't want to come up against another on national television.

"Rachel, tell me about yourself. I won't understand Martha's story if I don't know you a little better."

"That won't take long," she said. "I was born in New York. My father worked on the docks. He made good money, and we were by no means poverty-stricken. My parents were very much interested in my education. Education was the most important thing in our house when I was a child. Then the war in Korea broke out and my father was recalled. He never came back. We moved to Memphis, where my mother's family was from. I graduated from high school there, an all-black school, with a straight A average. My mother cleaned house for three wealthy families.

"I had a boyfriend. He was a year ahead of me in school and he graduated before I did. He had a job that paid him a lot of money, and he wanted to marry me. So, at the tender age of nineteen, I became a wife. My husband told me I didn't have to work. He wanted me to take care of our children. I had two sons by the time I was twenty-one.

"I never understood my husband's business. He told me he was a salesman, but he worked for himself. He said he bought various kinds of merchandise and sold it. He said he always sold it first and then had it shipped by the manufacturer which meant he didn't have to maintain an inventory. It sounded very good.

"But one day my world came apart. The police came to my house and told me that my husband and my twelve-year-old boy had been killed in a gunfight with dope smugglers. Brian, my fifteen-year-old son was being held in jail. Unbeknownst to me, my entire family had been engaged in drug smuggling. Brian was sentenced to three years in a prison for juvenile offenders. A month before he was to be released, another inmate killed him.

"I had nothing. My husband had always told me that one day we would retire and live in Jamaica. There was no estate, no insurance, nothing. I moved back to New York and ended up on welfare. I was forty-five years old. I started going to church for the first time since I was a child, and that changed my life. Then along came Martha Smith, and her tiny twins.

Whatever the world says about Martha Smith, she was my salvation. I now had a new family. To this day, she is the kindest person I have ever known. But what really happened to me was that I had a new love. I'm sure God made that happen.

"Martha was constantly thanking me for what I was doing. Some day, she told me, we would all live better, she and I and the girls. But at the time, it was hard to put food on the table or clothing on the girls. She insisted on giving things to me. I told her that was not necessary. I was a member of the family.

"Martha wanted to get away from where we lived. She kept trying. She worked nights, Saturdays, Sundays, holidays. In this way, she managed to make enough money to get off welfare and to move us out of the terrible place where we lived. She insisted I go with her; she said that she would earn enough money to provide for me, too. For my part, I could not walk away from her or from Michelle and Melinda. They were my family. We moved to an apartment building in lower Manhattan. A three-room apartment housed us all.

"The girls became attached to me. Their mother was gone almost all the time. I was their nanny, but they called me Nana.

"One day I heard Martha crying in the kitchen. I had just put the girls to bed and was listening to the radio. We had no television back then. Martha thought television a bad influence on children. Anyway, I looked into the kitchen and saw Martha with her head on the table sobbing. This strong woman was crying! I couldn't believe it! I went to her side and noticed the newspaper on the table. She'd been reading the sports pages. The headline read: JIMMY SMITH CRUSHES CHICAGO. Somehow I knew Jimmy Smith was the father of her children. I asked her, and she nodded. I leaned back and took her in my arms. For a moment I said nothing. She had told me that she was pregnant when she was divorced.

"I said, 'Martha, you must call him. Does he know about the children?'

"She shook her head.

"I said, 'Didn't you ever tell him he was the father of beautiful twin girls?"

" 'No,' she replied and would say no more."

Darkness was approaching. I turned on the office lights and called for a pizza. I could not abort the interview. I had to have the whole story now. "Did the girls have any idea of who their father was?"

Rachel drew closer to the desk. "I asked Martha about that when the girls were in first grade. 'No,' she said. 'I told them he'd died in Vietnam.' What she had done was update my father's story, and the girls believed it without question. They must have thought most fathers die in wartime."

"Didn't the children ask about their father?" I asked her.

"They never knew a father. They had no reason to ask about him. And if she had told them the truth, what would they have done with the knowledge? Should she have invited him to her home in that hellhole in Flushing, or in the second place we lived in, which was not much better, and said to them, 'This is your father.' Or should she have spent her last cent and flown to California and appeared on his doorstep to say, 'Hi, there! Here we are. Your ex-wife and your children.' Or should she have written him a long letter telling him that he should start assuming his responsibilities without it appearing to him and to his agent/counselor/advisor Walter Harman that she was blackmailing him, or trying to embarrass a big star? Maybe some meek, one-night hustler might have done that, but not Martha! She would take care of her children herself."

"But she could have told them when they were older," I declared after opening the door for the pizza delivery and clearing my desk of papers.

"She could have. I broached the subject again when the girls were graduating from high school. I thought how nice it would be for their father to witness their graduation. Do you know what she said to me?"

"No, what?"

"She said, 'When my daughters began asking about their father I told them their father had died before they were born, and in a sense this was true. Should I have told them he was too busy being famous to bother with them? That he had not bothered to ask about them before or since they were born? Should I have told them their father was a rich football player and movie star who didn't care if they had enough to eat?'

"I told Martha it wasn't fair for the girls to live out their lives not knowing their father. She looked into my eyes and her voice was harsh as flint. Her face was grim. 'I'll never go to him,' she said. 'I won't go begging for help. No one will ever say I blackmailed him. He knew I might be pregnant. He knew he might be a father. Never once did he write or call to ask how I was, or whether I'd given birth. He forfeited all rights as a father before his children were born!'

"I tried to calm her down. She was shouting, and I was afraid she'd wake the girls. 'Can you imagine what I'd have to deal with if I told them? What other questions would I get? What if they wanted to see him? We are a family of our own. He would be an intruder. Do you think he would have them visit him? What would happen to his image? Do you think he would come to see them once a week or once a month? Get real, Rachel. He lives in a different world, a world my little girls have never experienced, and if they were to experience it once in a while, would they be happy living the way they had been living? And if he started throwing money at them, what would it do to the values we've instilled in them? But this is just sheer speculation, because any real connection with his family would not be permitted by Walter Harman, his master. It would reduce Walter's commission and tarnish Jim's image as the most handsome bachelor in the world.'

"I remember that scene with Martha shouting at me as if it were yesterday," Rachel said, helping herself to another slice of pizza, "and the girls crying in bed, wondering what was going on. We ran in to comfort them and fell asleep, Martha in Melinda's bed, me in Michelle's. We never talked about it again, and I've never been sure whether she felt betrayed or was revengeful. Perhaps it was both.

"I did not try to change her mind. I knew what she had suffered. She had the right to do as she pleased. At that time I did not know about how she had made Jim into a hero. I didn't know that she had been urged to go to college to pursue a Ph.D. Meanwhile, he divorces her, gets on with the life she'd planned for him, and becomes a legend. It's not fair, but God never promised Adam it was going to be fair."

"How long did you live in Manhattan?" I asked.

"Four years. Martha, she worked all the time, seven days a week, night and day. And she followed Jimmy's career in a quiet way. She read newspapers, magazines, but she didn't clip them. Whenever she heard his name on the radio or in the casual conversation with other people, she would stop whatever she was doing and listen carefully. I caught her doing that a few times, but I didn't say anything. Then, when he became a movie star, it was worse. Was she still in love with him, I wondered, or was it hate? Martha always was inscrutable."

Although I was now trying to put a spin on a different kind of scandal, I believed that this complex woman was capable of conspiring to commit murder. Had she done so? Was her ferocious determination put to ruthless ends? Rachel's impressions of Martha Smith did not provide me with a definitive answer, but her keen insight painted an intimate portrait of a woman wronged, a woman determined not just to survive but to conquer.

16

We finished the pizza I had ordered by phone. It was dark and chilly outside, and clouds obscured the moon. I thought a storm was brewing but wasn't sure if I was sensing inner or outer weather. I sensed Michelle was nearby and to block the surge of loneliness, I asked Rachel how they got from New York to Lansing, from poverty to wealth. "I know Martha did it on her own, but how did she manage it?"

"Not that way you think. Martha was no financial genius." Rachel laughed. "When she couldn't make hard work pay off, she took a chance and got lucky."

"What did she do?"

"What she did was simple; a child might do it. You see, she got so frustrated reading want ads and applying for jobs she didn't get that she decided to place her own ad. It said, 'Job wanted by a well-trained person in secretarial, accounting, and real estate.' And with the faith of a child she spent more money than she could afford to run that ad in every metropolitan paper in New York City, Philadelphia, Los Angeles, Chicago, and Detroit. She ran the ad in the 'Help Wanted' section of the papers. The ad was no larger than the other ads but it had a black border around it."

Martha got just one response. A realtor by the name of Arthur Lake from Lansing, Michigan; said he was looking for someone like Martha, and he told her he would consider her for the job if she came to Lansing at her own expense. Martha decided they should all go: Martha, Melinda, Michelle, and

Rachel. They took a plane to Detroit, and in the terminal heard Martha's name being called, directing her to the baggage area. A man dressed in coveralls approached them. "You be Mrs. Smith?" he asked her.

Rachel thought the man evil, but she was always suspicious of anyone who did not speak grammatically correct. He said his name was Spencer, and he led them outside to a car with "Lake Realty" printed on it. Spencer was Lake's handyman, and he drove them to the company offices in Lansing—one hundred seventy-five miles north, helped the girls get out of the car, and grabbed Martha's old duffel bag. Rachel led the girls into the building, and Spencer carried the duffel bag into a small reception area where there was a single desk, two chairs, and a sofa. Nobody was in the room. Feeling jittery, Rachel started to pray, but Martha took her hand and said everything was all right.

Spencer left the room and, a few minutes later, a door opened and a man and a woman came out followed by Arthur Lake. He was tall and slender, forty-five to fifty years old, with a pleasant smile, well-dressed but modestly so.

Arthur Lake went to the girls and extended his hand to them. As he held Michelle's hand he remarked, "You look tired. Tell me if the sofa is comfortable." He led the girls to the couch, seated them, and then greeted Rachel. "I'm Arthur Lake," he said and took her hand.

"How do you do?" Rachel said and told him her name.

Finally he turned to Martha. "And you are Martha Smith." He held out his hand and flashed a big smile. "Welcome to Lansing." He invited Martha into his office, and Martha asked Rachel to accompany them, so perhaps she was not as controlled as Rachel believed.

Rachel hesitated, but when she saw the girls were falling asleep she joined them, happy to lend Martha whatever support she could. "You have gone to considerable expense to come here," Lake remarked. "I appreciate that."

Martha wasted no time. "Mr. Lake," she said, "I won't pretend. I need a job desperately. I want to go to work as quickly as possible. Please believe me, I can handle the job."

Lake smiled. "You don't even know what the job is." He wasn't handsome like Jimmy Smith, but his kindness and consideration more than made up for that, and he wasn't bad looking either, not that his looks mattered to Rachel or Martha.

Martha replied, "Mr. Lake, I can do anything in an office that needs doing."

He seemed pleased with her response. "According to your ad you're experienced in real estate sales, yes?"

Martha assured him she could be licensed in Michigan. "I'm ready to handle sales, reports, listing, whatever."

"Well, let me tell you about my situation," Lake said, looking out the window that dominated his office. "My secretary is retiring. She is available to show you the ropes, but she is not licensed as a real estate broker. That's a plus; I can use somebody with that qualification."

Lake started to say something, then got lost in thought, and after a moment of awkward silence, Martha said, "What kind of real estate? Residential? Commercial?"

"Hmm? What? Oh, residential mainly. Please forgive me. My wife suffers from multiple sclerosis. She is in a wheelchair, and I want to spend more time with her. We have no children. I have nobody in this office now that my secretary is retiring." For the first time, he met her gaze. "If you are willing to work, you'll have plenty to do. I'll pay you three hundred dollars a week and a commission over and above your base salary. Is that acceptable?"

All during her adult life Martha had to deal with people who measured her from head to foot. Was she sufficiently attractive? Why was Jimmy Smith stuck on her? How would she look in this year's fall fashions? Here she would not have to be a feminine showpiece. She could work and prove her worth.

Without hesitation, Martha told Lake that his offer was fair and she would like to start work as soon as possible.

"Not so fast," Mr. Lake said. "First, you'll have to find a place to live, unless you already have a place."

Martha laughed. "I'm self-confident, but not *that* self-confident."

"That's all right. I'll take care of that." He smiled at them. "You have a friend in the real estate business." He picked up the phone and said, "Please come to the office. I want you to show our new employee an apartment." Then he turned to Martha. "I assume you need room for yourself, Mrs. Strong and your children. Mr. Raymond will show you what we have available. In addition to other ventures, we manage two hundred fifty apartments in town. I'm sure we can find something you'll like. As for rent, the larger apartments rent for eight hundred and fifty dollars per month. You can't afford that now. So the company will pay your rent for the first month."

Ralph Raymond drove them to the L'Oreal Garden Apartments. Here was no red brick building eight stories high with graffiti spray-painted on the walls but a complex of single-story apartments around tailored lawns and flower gardens. The buildings were of white vinyl siding with windows which were opened by pushing them out, not by tugging them up and down. Inside was another treat. There was a spacious living room, with television and fireplace, a kitchenette with a dining area, and three bedrooms—sheer luxury. Maybe, Martha thought, their luck was changing. The two girls could not believe their eyes. They wandered around and around with big smiles on their faces. Rachel began to cry; Martha came over and hugged her. "It's a palace!" she whispered.

As if fate would not permit exuberance, Martha unfolded the newspaper she had picked up in Lake's office and was confronted with a photo of Jimmy Smith. The football star had made his first movie, and though the reviews were mixed it was a box-office hit! Jimmy had just helped his team win the National Football League title, and, the story went on, he was to commence work on a second new film within the month. The photo depicted him with a beautiful woman on each arm. Martha put the paper down and Rachel picked it up. Neither said a word.

The next morning Martha was at the office at eight o'clock. The door was locked, and she had no key. She went to a restaurant a short distance away and returned at nine o'clock. The office was now open, and a gray-haired lady greeted her. "I'm Edith Butterfield," she said. When she learned Martha's identity, she announced, "I'm retiring. In accordance with Mr. Lake's direction I'm here to show you the place." She proceeded to point to two file cabinets and a larger two-door metal cabinet. She told Martha the file cabinets contained all current files on rentals and sales as well as all current listings. The two-door cabinet held supplies, paper, pens, cleansing equipment, and other miscellany. She opened every drawer of the desk. They were all empty. She pointed to a clothes hanger and the door to a rest room. The account books were on a table beside the desk and she proceeded to show them to her, one by one. Rolled up and leaning against the wall next to the file cabinets were maps of the city and the county. Maps of other cities were on the desk. It was all very simple. There was an electric typewriter, a telephone, and nothing more. The office was quite bare.

She gave Martha her address and phone number. Then she added, "You will find Mr. and Mrs. Lake are very fine people. He has been a very good man to work for. He has looked after his wife while doing the best job he could. Now he wants to spend more time with her. You'll meet her soon; she is a very lovely woman. They have no children, you know. He often brings Hannah to the office in her wheelchair to acquaint her with the office and the employees."

"Who are the employees?" Martha asked.

"You, Mr. Ralph Raymond, Spencer, the maintenance man, and occasionally somebody to help Mr. Raymond. We have always been a close-knit group. Mr. Lake is not a tyrannical boss. He works along with his employees. Do a good job, and you'll be appreciated. Take shortcuts and he'll derail you."

Just then, Mr. Lake came in and Mrs. Butterfield left, telling Martha she was happy to have met her and wishing her good luck. To Mr. Lake she said, "I'm going, Arthur, I have a lot of things to do. If you need me for any reason just call."

17

So began Martha's career with Arthur Lake. From various sources and many interviews, I pieced together this story, which is better told directly than by quotes from others. She was ready, invigorated, determined. Rachel was now a permanent part of her household, a part of the family. Martha did not have to worry about the children. Rachel was in the apartment night and day. She could take the girls out of the apartment and into a garden of trees and flowers. There were swings and other playground equipment for exercise and entertainment. Martha could devote herself to her job fully.

She had no trouble obtaining a Realtor's license. There was reciprocity by which her previous license automatically qualified her. She got no further instructions from Mr. Lake. He simply went about his business as always. The first thing she observed was that there was not enough staff to manage and maintain 250 apartments while handling daily real estate listings and closings, but she did not think it wise to seek to employ more people as her first contribution to the operation. She reached Mr. Raymond by phone and reviewed with him the apartment operation. She found him to be a man in his forties, vigorous and pleased that she wanted to discuss management instead of repairs. She learned that he had been delegated to employ part-time people to do superficial cleaning. She and Raymond agreed that they would try to make permanent arrangements with some of these people so that there was enough help at all times. She determined that this would not entail much added cost, because

Lake was getting these people through a private agency and paying an hourly rate that was more than the employee was receiving. This difference covered social security, workers compensation, and a fee for the agency. Martha examined the records and found that though the same people were not always employed, the temps worked more than two additional full-time workers, and Lake was paying enough to hire three full-timers. Her computations showed that they could hire three people full-time and still save money. When she talked to Mr. Lake about this, she had Mr. Raymond with her. Arthur Lake had not expected this. It was not a part of a secretary's job. He was at first surprised and then very pleased. Mr. Raymond understood that Martha was worried that Mr. Lake would tell her this was not her responsibility and might even feel offended. She was afraid he might take it as criticism of the operation of his own business. He merely said, "Okay, let's do it. You two hire the people." That's all there was to it. But that day at 5 o'clock he called her on the intercom and asked her to come to his office. She was sure she had offended him.

His remarks startled her. "My name is Arthur. I'm generally called Art. I'd appreciate it if you call me Art and I'll call you Martha."

This was clearly not an approach to become familiar with him physically; he was simply a decent individual who wanted friendship not sex. She managed to say, "Thank you. I'll be very happy with that arrangement. I hate formalities."

"That takes care of that," he smiled. "Now, next I want to thank you for your suggestion about apartment management. I should have thought about that long ago. I want you to take over the management of the apartments. I admit I'm a little concerned about whether you will be able to do that and still be my secretary and sell real estate. Frankly, I wouldn't ask you to carry such a load, but apparently you like to solve problems and you discern problems quickly. We may have to hire somebody to help you. We will see what the future holds." With that, he got up and extended his hand. She grasped it but could not manage another word.

Of course she was delighted. She was also in a state of shock. This guy was a gentleman without pomposity or the macho tendencies she had so often encountered. When she got back to her desk she had to take a moment to clear her head. "Indeed," she thought, "my lucky has really changed."

In the days ahead, she went through the present listings and tentative sales, deciding to attack the listings first. She wondered, *How does one get more of them?* She studied the company's advertising, comparing theirs with other firms' advertising. Lake seemed to be last in the number of ads he was running. More exposure could help, but she also learned that advertising was very expensive. What was the alternative? Was there any way they could reach people more directly but less expensively? Telephone calls angered people. Mailings simply add to the junk mail. Unless one was buying or selling property there was no general interest in real estate. Some local firms had entered into ties with national organizations which provided the advertising on a national scale. Art Lake would not want that.

The more she thought about the problem, the more it became apparent that there was a difference between advertising and good will. "When people buy or sell a home," she told Rachel, "they want somebody they can trust, somebody who won't sell at any price or buy at any price just to earn a commission." People expected realtors to know values and follow them. More than that, lawyers expect you to make sure the property has no physical flaws. Here, then, was the avenue to follow to gain people's trust.

Martha was not concerned about commercial listings. If you made your reputation in residence, owners of commercial property would learn about you. She had other ideas for commercial listings and sales. It would be more details, take more time, but it should pay off well. But first and paramount was to gain the trust of the people.

Television was still a young medium, but it got right into people's homes. There was a problem of format. How should it be done? It occurred to her that television offered an opportunity for something programmatic that would hold people's attention. She thought of others who might be interested, particularly builders and banks.

She envisioned a seminar with experts in all fields that touched on home ownership, not just real estate purchases but repairs, remodeling, building, and financing. "The home is always the first adventure people get into," she told Rachel. "And it is an area where plenty of advice is needed." She talked to the manager of a local television station and learned the cost of putting on a half-hour program. Then she contacted banks, contractors, furniture and appliance dealers, repairmen, and city personnel who could speak on zoning problems. She found sponsors of a seminar on all phases of home buying and repair. Panelists would get valuable exposure. Martha entered into agreements with all the participants. This would be new. It would grab attention.

When she had all the details in place, she prepared a long memorandum and put it on Art's desk. She didn't hear from him until the following morning. He came into her office with the memo in hand and asked her into his office, closing the door behind her. She stood there, not knowing what to expect. He seated himself and asked her to be seated. Before he could say anything she told him this would not be a national hookup. That would be too expensive. They needed only local exposure, but local meant 300,000 people!

Lake said nothing, simply looked at her. Finally, he said, "Martha, I had planned to take it easy, stay with my wife. This program will be a bombshell. I spent the night thinking about it. I wasn't sure how to react, but I can now tell you that my first thought was to tell you that I wanted no part of it. I have never wanted to make a lot of money, but I simply cannot say that to you! You, my dear lady, are something special. There are not many people like you. How could I be so lucky as to have you in this office? You have been good enough to take a real interest in my business. Nobody else would have done that. They would simply put in a good day's work and go home to their own interests, but not you. My real problem is that I'm not able or qualified to join you in such an operation."

Martha had not expected such a speech, but she had an answer. "Arthur Lake, you have no idea what you have done for me and my children. It is my turn to do something for both of us. I don't care how little you want to be involved. I'll do it all!" Martha was in tears. She beat her fist on the desk. "So help me God, Art, this is my life. This will be the consummation of all I have learned to date. And you will be the beneficiary. You are the one who is special, but you cannot help being special. I need you. I need you more than you know." Her thoughts went back to the times she had been overruled because she was not pretty.

Lake said nothing for several minutes. He looked at her all that time, but his stare was not like that woman gets from men. He just looked into her eyes. His eyes transfixed her. He was not feeling sorry for her or shocked or disgusted. He was trying hard to understand her. He was a fellow human being who cared enough for her as a person that he could not tell her he had no interest in her project. He was thinking of her! He was concerned about her, not about himself. At that moment he became a dear, dear friend. Finally he said, "Okay, Martha, you go ahead with this project. I doubt you will need any help from me, but I'll be at your side if you need me. Let's see where we go from here."

Then she did something unintended. She took his hand and kissed it.

The TV program was an immediate success. It was the first of its kind and received a wonderful response. Half a million people now knew Lake Realty. Martha was amazed at the speed with which the business increased. A wonderful but unanticipated result was that the co-sponsors had joined with them in putting individual deals together. Lake Realty would secure the client wanting a new house. Martha would locate a lot, get plans from the contractors, interior decorators and furniture dealers. They would show this process on TV.

It was soon necessary to hire a secretary, because she was so busy preparing each TV show and handling individual sales. Arthur was astonished. Lake Realty became the biggest real estate firm in Lansing in a year, and in two years the largest in the state.

They were making more money than they had dreamed possible. Arthur bought a customized van in which Hannah could ride in her wheelchair and be lowered to get out of the van and lifted to get on. Martha built a new home under the program. It had 2500 square feet, more than twice the space of the apartment. Rachel had her own apartment with a separate entrance and with complete access to the rest of the house without having to leave the building. Martha bought a car for Rachel and one for herself.

In the next two years they became very close with Arthur and his wife, Hannah. They had meals together. They went out together, often to a park for a picnic, sometimes to places they wanted to see. All of them could fit in the van, which was customized to accommodate Hannah. Hannah, who did things that neither Martha nor Rachel had done very well, fell in love with the girls. She saw to it that they had the most attractive clothing. Rachel could drive the Lake van with Hannah and the girls and go shopping.

Hannah Lake was a well-educated woman. She read widely and she interested herself in the children's education. She determined their curriculum and their extra-curricular activities. She took over their education when the girls were in middle school and continued until both girls finished college, or rather until Melinda graduated, because Michelle quit when she was a sophomore to pursue acting as a career. Hannah involved herself in everything except church. The Lakes were not church-going people. Rachel took care of that.

Rachel took the girls to her church, a fairly large black church in downtown Lansing and taught them to pray. She took them to Sunday school in her car. Rachel recognized Hannah as an unusually well-educated woman who took an active interest in community affairs and she followed her lead, taking on the cause of educating disabled children.

Martha was overwhelmed. This was heaven. She could be with her children when she had time, and when she was not with them she knew they were in the hands of two very capable people. She was free to do her thing. She was proud to be providing for her children and for Rachel in a manner she had dreamed of but had not been sure she could manage.

18

The story of Martha Smith was becoming more interesting. Through various interviews, I had traced her through her divorce, the birth of her twins, through the hell of New York, and Lansing with Arthur Lake, the defendant. This was now in the spring of 1984. It was April, on a Monday, that I received a phone call from Moynihan. "We lost," he said. "The Court of Appeals has ordered a new trial."

"How did they manage that?" I asked.

Let me read their opinion. "We fully appreciate that the defendant's constitutional protection against double jeopardy must be given the strongest possible support. However, it is our opinion that if we accept the defendant's argument we will virtually abolish the instructions by the court to the jury. Each juror in this case, stated under oath that in the absence of other direct proof of the crime they would not consider circumstantial evidence such as the affair between the defendant and Ms. Smith. Such a position totally ignores the instructions of the trial court, which, incidentally, the defendant does not challenge. It also ignores the law. If we accept the defendant's reasoning, we will render all court instructions to a jury a nullity. The jury will make its own law. One wonders if, under such a system, we would use rules of evidence. We are not prepared to enunciate such a radical change in our judicial process.

"We direct a new trial."

The Supreme Court refused to hear the appeal.

Of course this was the time for Owens to publish the article she had shown me on Martha Smith. She wrote her lead: "Alas, the public was right, the jury was wrong." *Exposé* ran the article on its front page, the lead sentence in capital letters.

The *Exposé* story might not have made much of an impact had it not touched on Michelle Morgan, now a well-known star. In fact Michelle's name was put first in the stories appearing in the national press and magazines. And, of course, it was tied into the so-called affair between her and her father. The fact that a known movie star was a part of the family and the fact that Michelle's name had appeared in the story about her and her father, was too much for certain reporters to ignore. There did not have to be any connection, any relevance, between these separate incidents. The story, overall, was too juicy to leave untold—for whatever it was worth, if anything.

It was not more than a week after the *Exposé* article appeared that Michelle called me.

"I hate to bother you about this hateful thing," she said, "but I have to talk to somebody and you know more about all of this than anybody else I know. I called mother and Arthur and told them I loved them and that I was sorry about this thing. Once I told you that I did not want you to write about it. Now, I want you to tell me what we do now—and I do mean *we.* I've talked to Melinda and Claude. All of us are ready to fight this thing to the end. I need you. We all need you. Will you help us?"

"Michelle," I replied, "I'm the one who needs you." I could hear a gasp over the phone.

"What do you mean?" she asked.

"I mean," I said, "that I have taken on the task of putting together a defense for the new trial. I'm talking to a lot of people. You can help me reach people you know and you can tell me what you know. I'd like to talk to you as soon as I can."

"Mark," she retorted, "I had hoped you might come out to see me. I just wanted you near me. There is absolutely nobody out here with whom I can talk or just lean on."

I asked: "Can you possibly come out here? You could help me interview people. I'm beginning to learn something about your mother's struggle. I must know more. You could help me."

"I'll need to arrange things here. I think I can put off taping some scenes. I'll see what I can do. I can also be closer to mother. I know she needs me and so does Art."

I had put down the telephone on my call from Michelle for no more than five minutes when I got a call from Melinda. She and her husband were on the line.

"I've been talking to mother," Melinda began, "she sounds like she is a little weary. That's not like her. Is it that bad?"

For an instant I wondered why I was the one being called. I liked to think Michelle called because she was beginning to like me. But I could think of no reason why Melinda would call me instead of Rachel or Moynihan. There was no point in debating that question in my own mind. I could only tell her that we would have to try the case all over again. "I know that," she responded testily. "My question is: How will the new trial be any different? It seems to me that the Court of Appeals has ruled that Arthur is guilty."

"Not quite," I ventured. "The jury will be instructed to review all the evidence about the relation between your mother and Arthur and determine whether Art's love for your mother drove him to commit this horrible crime."

"But Mother admitted under oath that she and Art love each other."

"It doesn't necessarily follow from that fact that Arthur would kill his wife. In the new trial we must prove that both your mother and Art loved Hannah too much to kill her. It's our job in the new trial to prove that."

"Will mother have to testify again?"

"Yes, and so will you."

"I'm ready."

At that moment Claude Trudeau spoke.

"And I'll testify. I can tell that jury that Hannah Lake was the focal point of the whole family. Everybody admired and loved her."

"Let's hope," I continued, "that the court will let all of you tell what you saw and heard."

Claude went on, "There has not been one word of hate, jealousy, even the simplest problem in the relation of these three people. Arthur loved Martha and he also loved Hannah."

I could not help putting a damper on such talk. Of course I knew that was our case. But I had to say, "People often kill people they have loved all their lives."

Melinda told me I could call her when I wanted her to come to Lansing.

I reported these conferences to Moynihan. He suggested I get back to Rachel Strong.

19

In my mind I tried to summarize what I had learned from Rachel Strong about Martha Smith. I was particularly interested because all I had learned depicted a very strong, determined, intelligent woman who had indeed overcome the slings and arrows of misfortune.

According to Rachel, despite her success not a day went by that Martha did not think of Jimmy Smith. She could hardly help it because his name and face stared at her from the screen and out of newspapers and magazines. Rachel was convinced that Jimmy's success seemed to spur her on though she would never admit that. Often she and Rachel saw his picture with a beautiful woman and read about his short-term affairs she would remark to herself but aloud "I've got more than you have, Jimmy Smith."

In daily conversation with Rachel, Martha sometimes would remark how different Jimmy Smith and Arthur Lake were. Arthur was older, of course, and respectable, never flashy. Jimmy was insecure, couldn't understand that she loved him, thought that he was her pawn. Arthur Lake was no pawn. She could never control him and she was not interested in doing so, not because he was married to somebody else but because he needed nobody to control him.

One day as they sat at his desk in his office he said to her, "Martha, I like you because you 'fit,' if you know what I mean."

"It is easy to fit with you," she replied. "You take me as I am and trust me to do what needs to be done. I love you for that. And it's not just me. You care enough about other people to accept them with all their faults."

Lake cut her off. "You're embarrassing me. Let's go out to dinner. Flattery makes me hungry."

Martha, Rachel, Hannah, Michelle, and Melinda climbed into the Lake van. Arthur drove out to one of the better Italian restaurants. What Martha later remembered about that outing was Arthur's treatment of the girls. He took them over. She was a little jealous at first but when she saw how the girls reacted she was all smiles. He sat between the girls and went through the menu with them, explaining the terms with which they were unfamiliar. While they did not know what to order, they were happy that he treated them with dignity and respect. It was also obvious he was having a great time. These were children he and Hannah had wanted but never could have. Throughout the meal he helped them with the pasta, cutting the spaghetti so they would not have to wind it around their forks.

In her wheelchair next to Martha, Hannah whispered in Martha's ear, "This is so good for Arthur. He loves children and it's heavenly to have two such beautiful girls in our family after all these years."

Hannah had already taken to the girls as a mother would and now her husband was acting like a loving father. She leaned toward Martha and added, "And we are one family, you know—you, your children, Rachel, Arthur, and I. Our lives have been made happy and fulfilled since you came to us. Our future is bright and promising. This is something I didn't dare even to dream about." She took Martha's hand in hers and faced Martha directly. "Take care of Arthur. He is fragile. He loves deeply." Rachel saw and heard all of this and told me about it.

20

Immediately after my rather brief session with Rachel, still in April, I asked Melinda to come to Lansing. She and her husband, Claude Trudeau, came to my office with Martha and Arthur. I was anxious that the Trudeaus had full input in my investigation. I reported to them what I had put together to date, all of which they knew, and told them that they must talk to Moynihan before leaving. Of course, most of the time we talked about the *Exposé* article which had aroused everybody. We discussed a possible reply to the article. We got Michelle on the telephone so she could give us her thoughts.

As we talked about the Owens article and about the new trial Martha began to show signs of the weariness Melinda had told me she had noticed in her mother. We concluded that there was no way we could publish anything which would counter the Owens article. Any such response would simply add fuel to the fire. It was sad to see this indomitable woman begin to tire of this ordeal. Arthur thought it best to take her home. She was developing a migraine headache. As she left she said to me, "Talk to Rachel. She knows everything."

After Arthur and Martha had left I began quizzing Melinda and Claude. "First," I said, "I want to know more about you. How did you meet? What do you do? What do you know?"

Melinda replied, "We met in graduate school at Duke University. Claude was my professor, and the most charming teacher I'd ever had."

I asked Claude about his area of interest. "Tribal communities," he said. "Especially mating rituals."

"When men chose women by dragging them to the newest cave?" I asked.

"Well, you see," Claude said, "there were no discos back then."

"In our case," Melinda offered, "I clubbed Claude."

"Not exactly," Claude laughed, "I was looking for a bridge partner . . . "

"And I expressed great willingness to learn," Melinda concluded triumphantly. "Two months later we became engaged."

Then Melinda told me about her very unique marriage ceremony. There were problems. Five women had to be considered—of course Melinda was the bride so that took care of one woman. That left four, Michelle was the bridesmaid. That left three, Martha, Hannah, and Rachel. Martha immediately passed on making all the arrangements a mother usually makes. She acknowledged that she was a business woman, not a socialite. Rachel deferred to Hannah because that was the way Rachel was. She would be happy if Hannah were happy, and Hannah would be in heaven if she could arrange the marriage.

So, Melinda was the bride, Claude the groom, Michelle the bridesmaid, Martha the mother of the bride, and Arthur gave her away. Rachel hosted the reception. Hannah made all the plans, defined the role of each; she was in overall charge.

It was not a large wedding, Melinda's family and the Trudeau family, which comprised of his parents, his brother Phillip who was best man, two of Claude's sisters, and some cousins went. College friends rounded out the cast. The wedding was held at the local Methodist Church, and the reception at Martha's home.

"Where did you honeymoon?" I asked Melinda.

"We didn't. The day after the wedding, Hannah had to be rushed to the hospital. Her disease, which had been dormant for years, returned with a vengeance. She had difficulty controlling her arms and hands. The pain was horrible."

For more than ten years Hannah had endured her condition, with blissful remission relieving her now and then. But suddenly the pain was so intense that morphine was needed to alleviate it. The drugs ordinarily used to relieve multiple sclerosis—carbamazepine, or a combination of perphenazine and amitriptyline, or even phenytoin or baclofen—weren't effective.

Hannah remained in the hospital for weeks. Arthur would visit her during morning visiting hours each day, and Martha would go in the afternoon. In the evening, Rachel would see her. Melinda and Claude visited daily for a week, then had to return to the university but came back most weekends. Michelle was filming on location in Canada but flew in when she could get away. They all prayed for Hannah, but no one aside from Hannah herself suffered as much as Arthur. He felt her pain intensely, Melinda said, and could not bear her anguish.

Doctor Archer told Arthur that his wife could not tolerate more pain medicine, expressed surprise at the intensity of Hannah's pain, and hinted that she might be playing on his sympathy. "Such pain is not typical of multiple sclerosis," he told Arthur. Ordinarily, in multiple sclerosis, pain is intermittent, not continuous. Arthur was livid and might have struck the doctor had Claude not intervened.

A thought occurred to me and I asked Melinda where Martha stayed. "She tried to comfort Arthur and spent several nights with him, but it was difficult being in two places at once, so she moved in temporarily. "It was all quite innocent, I assure you."

I did not ask how she knew it was innocent, but Rachel must have seen the doubt in my eyes for she interrupted. "There was no hanky-panky going on. All any of us thought about was Hannah, and her struggle to survive. Arthur needed Martha. He wouldn't eat, wouldn't bathe. He was a crazy man. Martha did not want to leave Arthur alone. I saw the two of them sitting silently hour after hour. Sometimes he would cry on her shoulder."

With each day Hannah's pain worsened, but the doctors would not administer more pain medication. As her pain became worse, Arthur's pain increased. He tried to work to keep his mind away from Hannah's plight, but when Martha would look in on him at the office she would see him staring into space and know he was thinking of Hannah. When he could no longer bear the pain, he would call for Martha, and she would try to comfort him, hold his hand, talk soothingly to him or hold him in her arms. On occasion a secretary would walk in on them. What they made of what they saw they kept to themselves.

Unable to stand the pain, Hannah told Arthur she wanted to die. She wanted no life-prolonging ministrations. She prepared a will to that effect and she also signed a "Patient Advocate" power of attorney giving Arthur power to withdraw treatment even if that meant death.

Frances Wyman also spent time comforting Arthur. Indeed, the entire office became involved in Hannah Lake's pain. They were concerned about Arthur's health and also that of Martha. Business declined.

"Things couldn't go on indefinitely that way," Rachel said. Arthur kept asking Dr. Archer to do more to alleviate his wife's pain. Doctor Archer told him that with multiple sclerosis one never knew when the end would come. She could have another remission. But he warned against giving her too much sedative. That might kill her. This confused Arthur, and angered him."

"I don't want to listen to this again," Melinda said, rising. To Clause she said, "Let's go home. Rachel can tell Mark whatever he needs to know, but it makes me sick to think about Hannah's last weeks."

When they had gone, Rachel resumed her story, telling me how upset Arthur was at Dr. Archer for refusing to increase Hannah's narcotic dosage.

"I'm sorry," Dr. Archer had replied. "We must not induce death. We can only alleviate pain. Remember, this lady has had two remissions. Who knows what the future holds? It doesn't seem likely that a remission is possible at this stage, but you never know."

"I don't want her to suffer, and she doesn't want to suffer," Arthur pleaded. "Why must she be punished?"

"Because it is the law." The doctor was pleasant but firm.

"Look," Arthur said, waving his Patient Advocate's document in the air. "I have authority to stop this treatment."

"Again I'm sorry, Mr. Lake. That does not give you the right to increase the sedative to alleviate her pain."

"That's insane," Arthur almost shouted.

"That's the law," the doctor repeated. "An overdose may kill her."

"Doctor, you administer a certain amount of sedative to relieve her pain, even though she may die. Is that right?"

"That's right."

"And by how much will a larger dose of sedative accelerate her death? An hour, a day, a week?"

"I don't know. No one can answer that question."

"What is an overdose, Doctor?"

"That depends."

"On what?"

"On the condition of the patient."

"And her condition?"

"Is critical."

"And how do you know that she is not overdosed now?"

"What we have given her is within accepted medical standards."

"In other words the dose is small enough to make sure it will not be lethal."

"That's right."

"You are less concerned about stopping her pain than you are about overdosing her!"

That was when Dr. Archer suggested that Hannah was playing on his sympathies and Arthur tried to slug him. Fortunately, Claude stepped between the men and defused the situation.

"No wonder Doctor Archer was a hostile witness," I said.

"It surprised me when I heard about it," Rachel admitted. "But if you got more questions for me, you got to feed me first. I haven't had a thing to eat all day."

"Do you like ribs?" I asked.

"Is the Pope Catholic?"

"Ever eaten at The Sawmill outside Lansing?"

"Can't say as I have," Rachel sniffed. "I don't eat out much since Hannah passed."

"Well, if you haven't been to The Sawmill for ribs, you don't know how good pork can taste. Dominic bastes his spareribs in a hot sweet sauce that makes my mouth water just thinking about it."

"I do like ribs," Rachel admitted, "and I have heard good things about The Sawmill."

"What are you waiting for?" I said and gave her my arm.

I knew Rachel wouldn't have a harsh word to say about Martha, so when we were settled in the taxi, I asked her to tell me something else about Arthur that surprised her.

After thinking it over, Rachel said, "I shall never forget the day Arthur said his first prayer. It was on one of these picnics. Arthur had pushed the girls on the swings and was playing shuffleboard when I announced that lunch was ready. I called all to the picnic table. I asked Arthur to say grace. He was startled but he saw the girls lower their heads and fold their hands before them. He uttered a very brief prayer.

"When Arthur dropped us off after the picnic, I noticed that Martha was unusually quiet. When I asked her what she was thinking, she said that Hannah had told her that Arthur was not the tough business man he seemed to be. He was, Hannah had said, 'a fragile human being who could be overcome by love.'

"She asked me if I thought Arthur was *fragile*, and I said, 'I can't say. He seems to be a caring mn who adores his wife. He looks after her all the time. At the same time, he is a loving father to the girls. He doesn't seem to have a wicked bone in his body. That's not what I would call fragile.' The girls called them Uncle Arthur and Auntie Hannah, don't you know?"

"And what did they call you?" I asked after we'd been seated at a corner table in The Sawmill.

"They always called me Nana," she said proudly. "Still do."

Over dinner I learned that Arthur and Martha spent a great deal of time with one another, talking about business and family affairs. They wanted to be together as much as possible. It seemed to Rachel that their great success in business led them to love one another, "but not in the modern sense. People who pray together do not commit adultery," Rachel said, "and after that first prayer at the picnic table, not a meal went by without giving thanks to the Lord."

Although I was somewhat cynical about her correlating prayer with abstinence, I said nothing. Clearly, for Martha, her association with Arthur Lake was an exhilarating experience. For the first time in her life she was loved and appreciated for what she was. Old feelings of inferiority faded away. Whether she felt no remorse about loving a married man because her love was chaste or because what felt so good could not be wrong, Rachel was convinced that she loved Hannah as deeply as she loved Arthur, and I was in no position to contradict her. I knew pitifully little about love. I wasn't even sure that the ache I felt in my heart when I thought about Michelle wasn't due to jet lag.

Martha told Rachel that Hannah was a wonderful human being. Both were kind and generous and true friends. Hannah loved the children just as Arthur did, and Rachel was convinced that Martha cared for Hannah as much as she cared for Arthur. I nodded and gnawed on my spareribs, determined not to voice doubts that would alienate her, but Rachel picked up on my unspoken questions and said, "I don't think you believe people could be generous and kind without having ulterior motives."

Feeling exposed, I exaggerated chewing and pointed to my mouth to buy some time. After swallowing, I cleared my throat and asked Rachel if she ever suspected Lake's interest in the twins might be a ploy to get closer to Martha.

"Absolutely not!" Rachel said. Blotting her mouth with her napkin, she told me about the time Arthur asked Martha about the girls' father. It was a direct, simple question which called for a direct answer. Martha never thought the day would come when he would ask, and she did not reply immediately.

"Does it matter?" she responded.

"It does."

"Why?"

"Hannah and I have decided to change our trusts. We have nobody except you and the children. We previously thought it was not our right to know the father of your children. But before we change out estate plans, we feel we should know!"

According to Rachel, this really floored Martha. She had never thought about the Lakes' wills or trusts. She knew that they had no children or close relatives, but she had never considered her family as possible inheritors. True, they considered themselves a family group, but Martha had never thought beyond informal pleasantries into legal realities. She felt overwhelmed, beyond appreciative, and more out of love than concern for law, said, "Don't do that. We are a part of your family, but we don't want any financial desires to cloud our relationship."

"Surely," Arthur responded, "it should not surprise you that we want to do this. You and I, including Rachel and the children, have become what we had not even dared wish for."

Martha said, "Then it doesn't make any difference who their father is. There is no reason to be concerned about him."

"Be practical, Martha. Suppose you should die before we do. If Melinda and Michelle are under twenty-one years of age, their father will be sole parent and custodian."

As was so often true of Arthur, he had thought the matter through to its consequences under any and all circumstances. Martha had trouble saying his name out loud, but at least she said, "The father of my children is Jimmy Smith!"

"The movie star? Fancy that! Why only yesterday I read he was signing a new contract with Universal."

"I do not follow his career," she lied.

"Doesn't he know he has two beautiful daughters?"

"No."

"Do the children know who their father is? After all, they are almost teenagers. They must wonder."

"They think their father is dead, and in a way he is. He chose to divorce me. I was pregnant at the time. He never contacted me or made any inquiry about his progeny. There is now no place for Jimmy Smith in our lives! It is not a matter of his rights or the girls' curiosity. He would be an intruder. Particularly now, when we have merged our families."

"Well," Arthur went on, "I must tell Hannah. She must know. We will make special provisions in our trusts for the girls in the event Hannah and I survive you. Otherwise, you will serve as trustee for the girls."

"There is no need for you to do this," Martha said, "but it relieves me immeasurably." She threw her arms around him, held him tightly, and whispered in his ear. "What would we have done without you? I love you and Hannah. We all love you!"

He put his arms around her and told her her love was reciprocated. "That's something few people will understand," he said. "But we understand, and that's all that counts."

But Martha could not relax. More and more she involved herself in the business. The changes in the organization simply gave her more time to expand her operations. She was in great demand for appearances at conferences and more and more articles were written about the golden girl who rose from the ghetto of New York to become wealthy and powerful. What was surprising was that she had not accumulated her wealth in the stock market like other rich women. She had not used other people's money. In fact, she had done it without money. Many organizations named her the woman of the year. Her face graced the cover of four magazines in a single year.

21

Friday, April 15

By this time I was more confused than ever. I was sure, however, that to learn the truth I had to know everything about Martha Smith. I must understand her!

I decided to interview Lake's secretary, Frances Wyman. Perhaps she could give a better account of the affair between Martha and Arthur. Bluntly, I asked her, "How could Arthur carry on simultaneous love affairs with Martha and his wife? He doesn't seem the type."

If I'd hoped to catch the prim, silver-haired lady off-guard, I was unsuccessful. She smiled. "Remember, Martha was called by the prosecution, not the defense. The defense would never have put her on the stand. She was much too vulnerable." She pursed her lips and looked at me as if I had come to call on her daughter and questioned my motives. "In strictest confidence, you understand—and I've been informed you are to be trusted with private disclosures," she said, more by way of admonishment than acceptance, "I shall tell you about an incident I witnessed.

"One day I was about to go into Martha's office when I heard her crying. This was rather unusual, so I didn't go in. I waited, thinking she would soon stop crying. I had to see her on a critical matter, you see.

"Then I heard Arthur's voice. He was trying to comfort her and kept asking, 'What is it? What is wrong?'

"Sobbing, Martha said, 'I've got to get out of here. I can't go on like this. Hannah is my dearest friend. She does not deserve what we are doing to her. Betraying her is the last thing I would ever do.'

"This upset me, of course," Wyman exclaimed. "I had no idea they were having an affair, but what I heard certainly gave that impression." She looked away, embarrassed. "That's why I kept listening. I make no excuse other than that I was astonished. Transfixed, if you will. Then I heard Arthur say, 'If you and the girls leave, it would be cruel to Hannah and to me. We have told you that you are our family, that this is something Hannah and I have always wanted and never had. If you leave, you will break her heart as well as mine. You would betray your children a second time. You have denied them the love of a father. If you take them away from us, you will deny them again. Melinda and Michelle have become Hannah's life. They have prolonged her life. Besides, where would you take them? Who would replace Hannah in their lives?'

"Martha didn't respond for awhile. Then she said in a voice I could barely hear, 'I've thought about my children. I've also thought about Rachel. But, Arthur, I cannot be with you like this. It's not natural. I love you. I cannot go on forever loving you and not having you. But Hannah needs you even more than I do! I must leave you to her!'

"Arthur said, 'If you leave Hannah, it will kill her! How will you feel then?'

"In the end, of course, Martha did not leave. And they continued to live this strange, celibate life together."

"It's a touching story. Do you believe it?"

"I do."

"Then why didn't you testify to it at the trial?"

The secretary did not hesitate. "It was Mr. Moynihan's opinion that if I told this story the prosecution would argue that it was a tacit admission by the defense that Lake had arrived at a dead end. The situation could not go on forever. They would have argued that at the hospital Arthur got a chance to solve this problem. Give his wife an overdose of morphine. That would end her pain and he and Martha could then marry. That was already the prosecution's theory."

Miss Wyman was convinced that there was nothing unnatural or unethical in the conduct of Martha and Arthur. "Can you explain that?" I asked her.

She smiled. "Not to your satisfaction, perhaps. You're a young man; it might feel unnatural for you to love desperately and remain celibate." She looked away again. "I am fortunate never to have experienced desperate love, so I do not know how I might have reacted to its physicality when younger. My parents were good Catholics, and I like to think I have lived up to the standards they set for me. Of course, times have changed, but still sexual activity is not for everyone. Celeste Romano is of your generation, but I daresay she agrees with me. Go speak with her. Her office is next to Martha's."

"I might do that to satisfy my own curiosity," I said, "but the public won't buy it."

"That may be so," the lady answered, "and that's because the public has been so steeped in trash they cannot accept that in a three-cornered affair someone is not betrayed. Believe me, Hannah was not betrayed by Arthur or Martha, strange and unusual as that may seem."

"Did I hear my name mentioned?" The door was ajar and in the doorway stood a dark-haired, petite young woman who exuded quiet confidence despite being rather ordinary looking.

"We were discussing the evils of motion pictures, dear," Miss Wyman said.

"Come in," I said. "We were discussing whether someone may deeply love someone who's married, make no bones about it, but refrain from going to bed with him."

"Maybe guys can't, but women can," Celeste said. "I can."

I felt offended. "Men are no different than women," I huffed.

Celeste shrugged. "I wouldn't know."

"Mr. Pierce is a film buff," Wyman said. "That's where he gets his ideas."

"Now, wait a minute," I protested. "Just because there's a great deal of sex and violence in movies doesn't make filmgoers sex crazy and gun happy."

"I wouldn't know," Wyman said haughtily.

"Now, now," Celeste intervened. "I thought the issue was love, but I agree with Frances that Hollywood teaches us that sex is prelude to any relationship. If you ask me, that attitude cheapens love and diminishes the strength and beauty of a touch, a kiss, a meaningful glance. It's as if music without lyrics or poetry without melody were meaningless. Some people cannot enjoy food without a wine, a day at the beach without swimming, or responsibility without control. People who want it all right now strike me as gluttons." She colored. "Don't get me started."

We laughed and Frances Wyman said, "We don't have to; you're a self-starter."

This time, Celeste laughed with us, and I thought she was very attractive when animated, and I was thinking of this when I said, "I think many people tend to rush headlong into things they don't fully understand or appreciate. Sometimes, what's worth pursuing isn't apparent right away."

"Why *pursue* at all?" Celeste asked. "Passivity is a dirty word nowadays, but I think waiting is a virtue. It builds character. Look what it has done for Martha Smith."

"What's it's done for me," Frances Wyman said, rising from her desk, "is to make me late for lunch. I was hoping to do some shopping as well. This kind of weather always puts me in mind to try on a new hat. Easter's just around the corner, you know."

Since I was a victim of unslaked desire, I had a hard time accepting the placid perspectives of a couple of unmarried women. I phoned LA to make sure everything was on track and was skewered by jealousy when I once again discovered Michelle not at home. I left a garbled message on her answering machine about her scheduled flight. I couldn't help wondering where she was. *Playing with Hollywood's beautiful people,* I thought, rubbing myself in misery. Well, why not? I was nothing to her, simply a faked fiancé who was subject to dismissal any time.

I diverted my attention from Michelle by thinking about whether Arthur had poisoned Hannah "to end her suffering." I could not conclude there had been a love affair in fact without answering the "big question." Certainly the jury's decision was not helpful. They never considered the love affair. Had they done so, their verdict may well have been: "Guilty!"

It was certainly possible that Arthur killed Hannah out of love for her. She was, after all, tormented by pain. She probably wanted to die. Nothing unusual about that. Almost every day at many hospitals, a loved one is taken off life-support in order to die in peace. Who would call that murder? Ah, but if someone aids in another person's death, what is that? Jack Kevorkian sits in prison for doing just such a thing. Is that justified? To many people, Dr. Kevorkian is a hero. Yes, but what if he were in love with the wife of a man he helped die; that would certainly put things in a different light, wouldn't it?

Perhaps, if there had been no Martha, Arthur might be justified in helping end Hannah's suffering. Sex or no sex, Martha was very much in the picture. Had the question been put in that manner, the jury would have ruled Hannah's death a homicide, maybe premeditated murder.

Therefore, it didn't matter why Lake poisoned his wife, if indeed he did. Whether it was to win Martha or to ease his wife's pain, his action, if indeed he had acted, was unjustifiable. To the extent that Martha refused his advances, if indeed he made advances, on the grounds he was married to Hannah, or promised favor when Hannah was no longer around, Martha was an accomplice.

Harriet Owens and others thought Martha ruthless. Could I trust Rachel's account of Martha's meteoric rise? Where might I find an unbiased assessment?

Miss Wyman had suggested Donald Morton, head of the mortgage brokerage firm of Knight and McKenzie. I walked back to the parking lot behind the building to reclaim my car, and although there was still time left on the parking meter my windshield bore a ticket signed by Roxanne Weber. I would have felt better had I thought this was the final installment on my psychic debt.

I wasn't in a good mood when I encountered Mr. Morton, but he turned out to be a pleasant if unassuming person who was ready to answer any question put to him. In fact, he was eagerly happy to share his views, and it was evident that he had followed the case closely.

"I understand that you worked with Martha Smith and Arthur Lake in financing their purchases of real estate, is that correct."

Mr. Morton cleared his throat. "Essentially that is correct. Let me explain. We are mortgage brokers. We do not provide the capital needed for a project; we find that capital. We have many clients, among them insurance companies, pension plans, banks, foundations, and individuals who need to keep their clients fully invested. We help put together projects we consider good investments and, on behalf of our borrowers, we get one of our investors to advance the funds either as equity or as mortgages. We then service the mortgage for the investors. We are paid a fee by the borrowers and receive a quarter point from the mortgage holder to service the mortgages; that is, to take payments and to see that taxes are paid, repairs made and funds remitted periodically to the holders of the mortgages."

"Very interesting, I'm sure, but let's skip to when you first made the acquaintance of Martha Smith."

"Yes. So . . ." Mr. Morton cleared his throat and sipped from a glass of water. "For several years before Martha Smith came along I financed some projects for Lake Realty. One day she came into my office, announced she was with Lake Enterprises, and asked us to finance the construction of a warehouse that was to be leased to a manufacturer. The manufacturer was what we call a 'Triple-A' tenant. That, for your information, is the highest possible credit rating."

"I appreciate your telling me that," I said. "I always confuse it with the Automobile Association."

"That is another organization," Morton said, taking another sip. "We are not affiliated."

"I appreciate your telling me that," I said. "You don't give out maps then, do you?" I kept a straight face and waved at the maps on his wall.

He thought I might be pulling his leg, but the maps on his wall were prima facie evidence of something. "No, we do not give out maps," he said and took a very small sip of water. "At any rate, as I was running some numbers on my calculator Martha started wandering around the room. She is an attractive woman, and I found that somewhat disconcerting. We had road maps on the wall, plot plans, architectural drawings, that sort of thing, all over the office."

"Just as you do now," I said, ashamed of myself for taking advantage of his enthusiasm.

"We had more then. Anyway, she asked me, 'What's all this stuff about?' I told her they were plans for a shopping center. Shopping centers were all the rage back then."

"Still are," I ventured.

"Nowadays it's malls."

"The more things change, the more they stay the same," I said.

"Isn't that true?" Morton said, and this time I wasn't sure he was having a laugh at my expense. "At any rate, after we had completed the work on her loan, I happened to say that there were great opportunities for shopping centers in rural areas. The urban and suburban areas had already been gobbled up by people with a lot of money, but there had been little shopping center activity in the rural areas."

"Why would anyone want to build a shopping center in a rural area?"

"Market share," he replied.

"What's that?"

"Martha asked the very same question, and I explained that national retailers had to be sure they got their share of any new markets. By rural areas, I was referring to areas traversed by the new Federal Interstate Highway System. The 1956 Federal Highway Act provided for new super-highways which now carry twenty percent of all the traffic in the country. But they are 'limited access' highways."

"What's that?" I asked, intrigued.

"You are very much alike, you and Martha Smith," Morton said, and I wasn't sure I liked the association. "Limited access means that there are only certain places where you can get on or get off the highway. The idea was to find land next to an access which would have a potential shopping area of two hundred thousand or three hundred thousand people or more. Such potential shoppers need not be residents of the city or town at or near the point of access.

"People from twenty to twenty-five miles away can get on these super-highways and be in a hundred fifty thousand, two hundred thousand or two hundred fifty thousand square foot shopping area in a matter of minutes. Big corporations had built centers in the metropolitan areas but there still were opportunities in the rural parts of the country. When you have leases with national chain stores which must maintain market share, local tenants come in because the chains draw the traffic. When I explained this to Martha, she said, 'Can I get into this business?'

"I almost laughed. This is not for a woman from a simple real estate agency, but she was persistent. 'Are you asking for yourself or for Arthur Lake?' I asked.

"She ignored my question. 'How do I get in? Where do I start?'

"I could see she was not the sort of person who took 'No' for an answer, so I suggested she become a member of the International Council of Shopping Centers. My firm was a member, so I gave her the address and phone number of the headquarters. The rest is history."

22

Autumn 1986

Martha soon learned which retail chains throughout the United States were in expansion mode. She got the names and phone numbers of the marketing division of each chain as well as the head of their real estate and leasing departments. She obtained and enlarged road maps of the new highways. She contacted the chamber of commerce in each town as well as the superintendent of schools, directors of hospitals, city managers, county executives, and tax assessors. She got the zoning maps for many of the counties and cities. She also contacted the highway departments on the state and county levels and learned the tax rates, including bonded indebtedness. She got from the chambers of commerce a list of all manufacturers in the area, number of employees, the average wage rate, and the quality of the fire departments, hospitals, and schools.

She confined herself to just a few states: Illinois, Michigan, Ohio, North Carolina, and Florida. She did not try the east or west coasts, at least not at first. Even so, this involved a tremendous amount of work.

For the most part she worked with local real estate men to obtain options on desired locations. She got several without too much expenditure. Usually she paid the going price for farmland, the value of which increased at least tenfold when appraised as part of a shopping center. She applied ten percent of the total cost of a million-dollar center as the value of the land; that is, one hundred thousand dollars. Sometimes leverage was twenty to one, depending on the strength of the location.

Martha then made agreements with local realtors to manage the affairs of a center, including maintenance, rentals, and taxes. Rent payments were forwarded to Enterprise Properties, a company she formed to develop and operate these centers.

Her income from the real estate agency was not enough to finance the building of shopping centers. To overcome this obstacle, she worked with options to buy land as well as options for leases. These all had a time limit. On paper, with options, she had five centers located in Michigan, Indiana, and North Carolina. She got bids from contractors with twenty-to-fifty thousand-dollar leeway in estimated cost. She was under enormous pressure. The leases would become void if construction was not started in six months.

She worked night and day. Morton's firm committed to the financing, but their commitments had time limits beyond which the lease options would expire. The idea was to sell three or four centers before construction actually began. After the leases had been arranged and the construction contracts signed, Morton sent her to see John Hulbert, CEO of Temple Investments in Detroit. "He's a willing buyer. Go see what you can do." I got a graphic story from Martha on what happened next.

A fat man who fancied himself a protector of women, Hulbert smiled patronizingly at Martha and told her to leave all the papers with him. "I'll discuss your project with Mr. Morton when he comes to town. You don't worry your pretty little head about any of this."

Tearing the papers from him, Martha stormed out. Returning to Lansing, she accosted Morton in his office at Knight and McKenzie. "Donald, how could you have sent me to see that pig?" she demanded furiously.

"Calm down, Martha, calm down," Morton said, raising and lowering his hands as if he were sending imaginary smoke signals. "Tell me what happened." Martha described the meeting, but Morton had a hard time seeing what was wrong with Hulbert's behavior. "He was only trying to help you," Morton said, wringing his hands.

"I won't be condescended to, Donald," she snapped. "Not by that man and not by you." Arthur would have understood, but he was caring for Hannah, who was recovering from the flu.

"I'm not being condescending, and I don't think Roy Hulbert was either."

"Why wouldn't he tell me if he accepted the sale price?"

"He wanted to discuss it with me first."

"I know that, but why?"

"He probably wanted to make sure financing was in place."

"I told him it was. He could have negotiated a tentative agreement contingent on satisfactory financing. That's when he told me not to worry my pretty little head about it, and I wanted to tear his head off. Did he think I would give him an option to buy without a price being agreed upon first?" She tossed her head defiantly. "Pretty little head, my foot! It might take six weeks or two months before the two of you get together, even longer before he decides whether to buy. I don't have that kind of time!"

"I'll speed things up. I'll call him this afternoon."

"I won't allow Mr. Hulbert to dictate the conditions of the sale."

While Morton and Hulbert got along well with one another because, consciously or unconsciously, they shared the same basic values, to Martha he was a pompous old man who was convinced that a woman had no place in the industry, and he was not going to waste his time talking to a woman who did not know what she was talking about. "He's not like that, really," Morton promised.

"The hell he's not! I won't do business with him." Morton was surprised to find in Martha a tough business woman who could tell somebody to "go to hell," and he gained new respect for her. In time, he sold four of her centers. Martha kept one. With the money she got for the four she sold, she only had to borrow about thirty percent of the cost of the center she kept. That center provided between seventy-five thousand and one hundred thousand dollars cash flow annually.

Feeling he'd been locked out, Hulbert became an outspoken enemy. He was not the only one, as Harriet Owens discovered while doing research for her story for *Exposé* Magazine.

Not long after the first centers were built and sold, Martha called on Don Morton with plans for a new shopping center, much like the ones she had already built. The timing was right, for a wealthy surgeon who was the client of one of Morton's partners had been complaining that very day about having to pay most of his money to the IRS for taxes. He wanted a tax shelter so he could keep more of what he earned, and he wanted it before the end of the year. McKenzie sent Dr. Kenilworth to Morton, who talked to Martha and arranged a deal whereby the doctor would provide eighty percent of the construction costs and act as owner of eighty percent of the property. With that equity, he could shelter nearly all of his income from his medical practice.

Shortly thereafter, trouble struck. First, the air base which employed five thousand people was closed by the government. Then the construction was delayed by bad weather and could not be completed within the time allowed by the leases. Moreover, additional money was needed to repair damage done by the rainstorm, and when the center was completed there was not enough income to keep it going. Martha asked Dr. Kenilworth to put up more money. He refused, saying that was not part of their agreement. "I put up the money to construct the damn buildings, and I'm not going to put up another red cent!" Fortunately, the anchor stores stayed, and the banks providing the money also stayed. But there were too many vacancies for the shopping center to operate at a profit. In fact, it was a deficit operation. Martha subsidized it and kept it going while continuing to demand that Dr. Kenilworth come up with his share of the money. After all, he owned eighty percent of the project. Finally, Martha had to sue him for eighty percent of the deficit, plus damages.

Kenilworth's lawyers advised him to come up with the money, but as the doctor was about to comply, the income tax code was amended. Now he would have to participate in the management of the center if he was to get his write-off. This he could not or would not do. He refused to shoulder his financial responsibility, so Martha offered to buy him out for an amount the doctor deemed paltry. He was finally persuaded to accept her offer when his accountant pointed out that if he got more money he would be subject to recapture charges and higher taxes.

Martha took over the center. Pretty soon the three anchor stores were drawing so much traffic that the establishments that had previously dropped their leases came back. And at a higher rent! Then, manufacturing plants and warehouses took over the former air base and began providing some employment. Martha was able to refinance the center for much more than the original mortgage because of the increased revenue. She got back all the money she had put into the center as well as what she had paid the doctor. In effect, she became an owner without any investment on her part.

Upon hearing of this, the doctor grew angry. He told people he had made a gift of almost five hundred thousand dollars to Martha Smith, who froze him out. He was supported in his assessment of Martha Smith by Roy Hulbert.

And so Martha Smith began to amass a fortune. Arthur was an equal partner in her ventures, Rachel told me, but whatever he owned was really a gift from her. In fact, before she came, Arthur Lake had what amounted to a one-man real-estate agency with an average or slightly better than average income. In her first five years, Martha increased his business by four hundred percent. In her second five years, she grew their business into a hundred million dollar corporation of which he owned half.

Wealth, however, did not mean acceptance either socially or in business, and Martha was determined to be accepted, if not on her terms, then, well, she was willing to give ground, strategically, as might a general who upon surveying the field before a battle pulls back to fight from higher ground. There were setbacks, at least two after that encounter with Hulbert. In one instance, she called the Dalman Company, a variety store chain, successor to an old five-and-dime store. The Dalman Company was only ten years old but well financed and in expansion mode. Martha had two locations she wanted to discuss with the vice president for real estate. She had her secretary make an appointment for her, but when she presented herself at the agreed upon time and place she noticed consternation on the receptionist's face followed by a flurry of activity, as if a rooster had invaded a henhouse.

A dour lady entered the reception room where Martha was seated and neither smiled nor took the proffered hand. "I'm Ethel Ward, Mr. Bradshaw's secretary," she said. "What can I do for you?"

"How do you do," Martha said pleasantly. "I have an appointment with Mr. Bradshaw."

"Mr. Bradshaw is tied up," his secretary said. "Perhaps I can help you."

Martha did not want to talk to the secretary. Her face fell, but she caught herself, smiled and said, "I'm interested in leasing space in some new shopping centers."

Ms. Ward hesitated, then said, "We are not signing new leases at the present time."

Martha knew this was untrue, but she calmly said, "I learned at the meeting of the International Council that you were signing new leases."

Ms. Ward closed her eyes the better to think, then explained, "Oh, those are old leases we are just getting around to sign."

"Yes. I'd still like to meet Mr. Bradshaw to discuss future plans for new shopping areas. I'm sure he will be interested. We told this to the receptionist when we made the appointment."

Ms. Ward's eyes flashed as if to say, "You, developing shopping centers? You expect me to believe that? Bug off! We don't have time for you." But aloud she simply said, "I'm sorry."

Martha tried several other approaches, but Ethel Ward's job as she saw it was to protect Mr. Bradshaw, and she performed her job well. Martha did not see him then, or ever.

The same thing happened when she went to a large food chain. Martha was not given to paranoid fantasies. She refused to believe that doors were closed to her simply because she was a nondescript woman in a man's world. Many companies had not yet learned that reaching out into rural areas was necessary if they wished to maintain their market share.

To counter their short-sightedness, Martha carefully prepared a presentation to show them how demographic and traffic flow influenced buying patterns. She didn't get a chance to make her presentation. A matronly woman took her by the arm and led her out the door, saying, "It's simply impossible to see the vice president today or any day."

Back in her office, Martha took stock of her situation. If she could only get in the door, she felt, she could reach an agreement that would benefit both parties. Her letters were good enough to get her invited to the office of potential customers, but when she made her appearance she was turned away without an explanation. Was it possible that her appearance turned people off? If so, she could save both time and money if she included a photo of herself in her correspondence. As she thought of this ridiculous stratagem, her mind's eye turned to the women she encountered on her trips. The women who looked like her were custodians. Those who had desk jobs were trim, well coiffured, and well dressed.

"I am what I am," she confessed to her mirror. "I'm not glamorous, and I don't know how to make myself any different. I'm color blind and I don't dress to attract men." On the one hand, she accepted herself for who she was; on the other hand, she was furious with the way things were. She felt insulted and wanted to fight it, but this was a man's world. Fighting would only make matters worse. She was playing a man's role and that was not allowed. Oh, there were many women who held high positions in this man's world, but she didn't look like any of them.

The twins paid more attention to what they wore and how they looked, thanks to Rachel and Hannah, but she had dismissed Hannah's efforts to get her to wear pastels and form-fitting dresses. She owned one evening gown, a simple black affair, and loathed wearing it. Thinking about it made her moody. Anger gave way to sadness, and she felt despondent, worthless. The feeling was so unusual, she was sure she was coming down with something and spent half the day at home staring out the window and waiting for the onset of illness before sheer boredom drove her back to the office.

She was busy enough. It was not that she didn't have work to do. It just irked her that she was not accepted the way men were accepted. An inner voice told her to take her children and leave, go somewhere or do something where she would be better treated. Another voice told her to stop feeling sorry for herself, to stand up and fight. That had always been her way. When the man she considered the love of her life had left her, she clenched her fist and got over it. She had attained financial success despite overwhelming odds, and for what? To find another man who was the love of her life, a man she could never have? What a joke!

23

At this point in my study of Martha I could see a very complex woman. I had heard of her love, devotion and loyalty. I had also heard of her quick temper, her determination, and what I have chosen to call her resourcefulness, which others were prone to call double-dealing. I pondered the words—resourceful and shrewd. Did one of these have a complimentary connotation and the other a despicable meaning?

I was sure Martha Smith was not a crook. I was not so sure that her determination to get what she wanted was limited in any way. Would she drive a man to murder? Of course, I had nothing to show that she manipulated Arthur in any way. However, that was not the point. The point was that what I was learning about Martha Smith could be considered as evidence of a capacity to destroy someone who stood in her way to get what she wanted most.

I was saddened that I had to see Martha in this possible role. My problem was that I had been seeking facts which would indicate that neither Martha nor Arthur would kill Hannah and what I was finding was that the fact could be construed either way—for guilt as well as for innocence. Arthur was appearing to be nothing more than a helpless pawn. Martha was the dominant character. She could very well have called the shot in the murder of Hannah. She was capable of deceiving people, as I saw it.

While pondering all of this I received another call from Moynihan.

"Can you come over?" he asked. "I've got to talk to you."

I went to his office immediately. As I entered his office he said, "the judge wants to have a pre-trial hearing next week. He wants to get a list of witnesses, discuss the issues and set a trial date. Are we ready for that?" he asked me.

"Not quite," I told him. "I'm learning a great deal about your clients. The sad part is that while I think what I have learned should be helpful to our case, I'm afraid the story is of such a nature that the prosecution can argue the facts I have assembled are proof of guilt. This case revolves around Martha Smith. Lake is just a troubled man in love with two women. But Martha Smith is both a loving person and a determined hardheaded, self-centered gal who will go to any end to get what she wants. She is no passive lady in waiting. She consumes men."

Moynihan asked: "Do we dare put Lake on the stand? Maybe it is getting down to the point where we must let the jury decide whether to believe him or Doctor Archer and his theory of the cause of death."

I had thought about that alternative. "If we put Lake on the witness stand he can deny that he put any morphine into his wife. If he does that, he must answer a lot of questions he can't answer. Where was he at the time of the alleged injection? If he says he was home, we are dead. Everybody saw him at the scene of the crime. If he says he only put two or three milligrams into his wife we run into the fact that the urine showed more morphine than that and even though that is not sure it is enough to discredit a guy whose life is one the line."

"But if we don't put him on the stand this time the jury may instinctively feel he is hiding behind the Fifth Amendment." With those words Moynihan tossed his pen on his desk as some sort of token of his dilemma.

"Should I try to get this pre-trial hearing put off to give you more time to investigate?" Moynihan finally asked.

"I think it would be smart to postpone the hearing, if you can, but I can't promise anything new or different."

As it happened, the circuit judge who was to hear this new trial, Henry Carter, became ill and the pre-trial had to be postponed. No future date was set.

Before continuing my so-called investigation I decided to talk to Moynihan to see if we could determine what information would be most helpful. We had no expert witness to contradict Dr. Archer. We could not answer the claim that Lake wanted to give more morphine to his wife even if it killed her. More than one person had heard him say so. We were caught in an impossible situation. Only Lake could explain his demands for more morphine for his wife. If he took the stand he would be asked if he did, in fact, inject his wife with more morphine. He had to admit he did or he would lose all credibility. If he admitted that and claimed he did not give her twenty milligrams, what had he done with the vial with the remainder of the morphine? If he admitted he had thrown it in the trash, he was admitting destroying evidence injurious to him. If it was not injurious why had he thrown the vial away?

At the pre-trial hearing Moynihan must decide whether Lake was to testify.

This was indeed a case which could break one. When you are sure the accused is innocent but the evidence would make it appear he is guilty, just how is he to be defended, if at all? There could be no plea of guilty on manslaughter because we knew Lake was not guilty, period! At least that was now our innermost thought, in spite of the evidence to the contrary.

24

I was becoming almost desperate. I seemed unable to find anything which would be helpful to the cause. I had pretty well uncovered all there was about Martha and Arthur. There was one aspect of the woman which still puzzled me. How or why had Martha been transformed from a homely woman to a beautiful one. It had seemed to me that it could not have been simple dieting. I remember Moynihan's remark that her transformation was "another story." So, there must have been something special. In my talks with Rachel I had learned how repeatedly Martha had been turned down by prospective investors, as she thought, nobody believed such a relatively unkempt woman could do what she proposed to do, how she had become almost morose about it. I had to learn more about that. I went back to Rachel.

"Martha got to a point where she had options for land purchases and leases which were about to expire and she was being turned down time after time. I wasn't thinking so much about the potential financial problem as I was thinking about her very life. I thought about how my minister, Joshua Hall, had helped me when I was despondent. I had to get Martha to him, somehow. On Sunday at breakfast when the girls were ten years old I suggested that she go to church with the girls and myself. She said she could not do it. Melinda exclaimed, 'You never go with us.' That persuaded Martha to go. I had already alerted Reverend Hall and told him of my concern about my dear friend.

"I told Martha my church had few white members. That didn't bother her. After the worship service, the girls dashed into Fellowship Hall, where the congregation and the minister gather after the service. Coffee, tea, and cakes are served, and people get to know each other better. I introduced Reverend Hall to Martha.

" 'I've heard a great deal about you from Rachel,' the pastor said, 'and your two girls are a delight to have around. Rachel is an old friend of mine. She asked if we might have a chat in my office. Come this way.'

"I'm sure Martha thought this would be about her children. She followed Reverend Hall into an oak-paneled room off Fellowship Hall. Rachel took up the rear, as the girls ran off to talk to friends of their own age.

"When we were seated at a round discussion table, Reverend Hall said, 'Rachel is concerned about your state of mind and hoped I might offer some suggestions. Now, I wouldn't think to meddle in your affairs, but I've children your age and grandchildren not much younger than your girls. I've seen a lot and heard a lot and if you care to listen, I'd be pleased to share some observations.'

"Martha gave me an exasperated look which said, 'You tricked me into this!' but she sank in her chair, prepared to listen.

"I said, 'Martha, I have been worried about you. We all have, Mr. and Mrs. Lake, and your daughters, too. I felt you should talk to somebody outside the family. You're all bottled up, Martha. To hear you talk, everything is fine, but on the inside you're crying. Sometimes it leaks out, too. Don't tell me different. I know you too well."

" 'I've had a few setbacks is all,' Martha said.

" 'More than a few setbacks,' I said.

"Martha faced Reverend Hall. 'What's frustrating is that my difficulties don't have to do with my ability but with the way

I look. To be blunt, my appearance turns people off. I can't talk to potential customers because they take one look at me and decide I am not capable of doing what I propose to do. My face gives me away. The impression is always the same. I'm a silly woman who makes impossible promises she can't possibly deliver.'

"To her surprise, Reverend Hall chuckled and slapped his knee. 'If that's your problem, you've come to the right place. I'm very well acquainted with the problem. I encounter it every day. I have five hundred members of my parish with the same problem. You are very lucky.'

" 'Lucky? How?' she asked.

" 'You are white. My parishioners are black. You can do something about your face. They cannot. Mrs. Smith, I am an ex-boxer. I was in the Olympics. I know something about conditioning. We take boys off the streets and we put them into good condition and make boxers out of those willing to make some sacrifice.

" 'Now, don't get me wrong. I'm not going to suggest you take up boxing, but I am going to suggest you join one of those health clubs which are so popular now and knock off forty-five or fifty pounds. After that, you might wish to consider some plastic surgery. It's really a simple program. All it takes is determination.'

"Martha's mouth was open, but no words came out. She was almost in a state of shock. There had been reasons for rejecting what Reverend Hall was suggesting, but they were buried in the past, buried with her love for Jimmy Smith. 'Well, I don't think . . . ' she started.

"Reverend Hall laughed softly. 'Then don't think. Now, I am no physician. I only know physical conditioning, but I have seen what cosmetic surgery, along with physical conditioning can do to a person's self-esteem. It will make a new woman out of you.' "

Driving home from church with Rachel seated next to her, Martha looked straight ahead and said, "Rachel, I love you."

"I know that," Rachel said. "You don't have to tell me that."

"But I do have to tell you. I hadn't thought, dear Rachel, that you have suffered worse abuse than I ever have and have never said a word about it. People without an ounce of your character and integrity have looked down upon you, and you have responded with kind forgiveness. Stupid people who have no idea that love knows no color have treated you as a servant and dared to give you orders, and you have closed your eyes to their ignorance and not rebuked them for their prejudice."

"That would only have stirred them up," Rachel said, tears in her eyes.

"There's not an ounce of self-pity in you, Rachel, and I've been wallowing in it. I have had the means to do something about my condition, and I have done nothing. Well, thanks to you and your pastor, I will do something. If it is the last thing I do, I'll fix myself. I'll do it for both of us."

"Oh, my, Martha, how you talk! Don't you worry about me. I can take care of myself. But I'm so happy for you. You've got your fighting spirit back!"

Joyce Eldredge, Martha's personal trainer at the Ajex Health Club, had never met a person under fifty with such poor muscle tone. "What's the furthest you've ever walked?" she asked Martha.

"Walk? I drive."

"Not any more, you don't."

"That's ridiculous. I live five miles from my office."

"Perfect," Joyce said.

"I leave for work at seven in the morning."

"I guess you'll have to leave at five, then."

Martha didn't even know she had muscles. By her third day of training, every muscle in her body ached. Had she told

Joyce how much she hurt, her trainer might have eased up, but Martha gritted her teeth and plowed on. Joyce was amazed at her determination, her dedication. It seemed that the more pain she felt the harder she worked. She rode the exercycle with a vengeance; she walked on the treadmill as if it were the road to heaven. Joyce had to slow her down. Martha attacked weight reduction as if it were a business deal she had to close, whatever it took. Aerobics punished her; she invited the torture. Never in her life had she done pushups, used a Nautilus machine, lifted weights and stretched her body as she had her mind.

25

On Monday, April 18, 1984, I received a phone call from Michelle. She was most anxious to talk to me. It was a call which will be forever etched in my memory.

"Mark," she almost cried, "please forgive me for bothering you. I just had to talk to you. Since the appeal of Arthur's case it has been miserable for me. All of the papers are writing all those stories about my mother and Arthur Lake. My name is in every one of those articles. Everybody treats me different now. They have made a sort of object of me. You would think that scandal is commonplace out here. Well, it may be, but it is not commonplace with me. I can't talk to anybody about anything. It's horrible. I'm calling you because I can always talk to you. Melinda and Claude talk to me by telephone, but I really need you. Please understand."

"Michelle," I replied, really delighted with this particular twist. Whatever misery there was in this series of events it was bringing her closer to me. "I'll be out there as quickly as I can get there. You don't deserve any of this. Have you talked to your father?"

"I can't talk to him. He's not my father!" She was now crying. "He is Jimmy Smith. I used to go with him. My father is Arthur Lake. And they are trying to put him in prison for life. That can't be."

"I'm leaving right away. I'll be with you tomorrow," I told her.

And then came words that were dear to me. "Thank you. Thank you. I'll be waiting for you. Melinda and Claude are also coming. I need all of you. But I need you most, Mark. You make all the difference."

When I got off the plane at Los Angeles, Michelle was at the runway from the plane into the waiting area. I went to her and took her into my arms and she kissed me. At the moment I only wanted to hold her. But we were holding up a line of people coming off the plane. Usually Michelle had someone with her. She was now enough of a celebrity that she needed protection. But today she was alone. We found a seat and sat down.

"Claude and Melinda are at my apartment. They offered to come with me but I told them I wanted you to myself. You have no idea, Mark, what you mean to me." She pulled me to her and kissed me again. All of this was heaven to me.

Michelle's apartment was really a condominium in a large, rather luxurious condo complex in Malibu. She had driven to the airport and we were quite a while getting to our destination. All of the time she was driving she told me about her life. Her agent was having problems. She had employment, but it was not what it should be. Somehow, the "case" was having a serious impact in her job opportunities. It was not simply "the case," it was also the affair with her father—something she had overcome but which came to life again as soon as it became known there was to be a retrial. "It's so disgusting," she said. "That so-called affair with my father has nothing to do with the case. But reporters can't write about the case without pointing out that Jimmy Smith is my mother's former husband and for some time he was my companion, as well as my father. It is not that my friends have turned their backs on me. They just don't know how to take me. They are reserved. They don't talk about my problem but it is always there. It's in my career that I'm having trouble. Producers are afraid of me—or of my problem."

At Michelle's home Melinda and Claude greeted us with open arms. There were only the four of us. Michelle had asked her maid not to come in. After embraces all around, Melinda announced she had prepared coffee and some "goodies." She seated us in the living room and went into the kitchen. Soon she was back with a tray of coffee and cake. "Claude, darling, will you get the other tray?" she called, and Claude went into the kitchen and brought out the other tray.

Melinda spoke first, "Mark, we are all ears. We depend on you. Where do we stand?"

I was hesitant to speak. There was nothing I could say which would alleviate the tension.

"Moynihan plans to have all of you tell it all—from the beginning to now. You two are going to tell the jury the story of your mother's struggle to keep the family going. You are going to tell about the family you had formed among you, your mother, Art and Hannah, and Rachel. You are going to tell how Hannah took you over and helped to educate you, how deeply she loved each of you and you loved her. We are going to try to show a love among all of us in which it would be unthinkable that Arthur Lake would deliberately kill his wife."

"That's the way it was," Melinda chipped in.

"I've learned that from my investigation," I replied. "The problem is that when we have told all, the prosecution is going to say 'You see, it's just as we told you. Arthur Lake loved Martha and he loved his wife. But it could not be that way. It happened that his wife was gravely ill and in great pain and she wanted to die. The way to solve the problem was to put Hannah out of her misery.' "

"That's horrible," Michelle exclaimed. "Uncle Arthur loved Hannah, worried about her all of the time. Sure, he loved Mother. That doesn't mean he would kill Hannah. We all loved Hannah. She was the center, the life of the family."

"I'm afraid that's the way the case shapes up. It will be up to the jury. They will decide. We must show the real love you all showed," I replied. "It's our only hope."

Claude asked, "Will Arthur testify?"

"When I last talked with Moynihan, he said he was going to list Arthur as a witness but decide at trial whether to call him," I explained.

Claude asked again, "Can't the prosecution call him?"

"Art cannot be forced to testify," I told Claude.

26

At the pre-trial hearing which I attended with Moynihan, I noted that Traver had listed no new witnesses. He was relying on the evidence he had presented at the original trial. But Moynihan listed Martha (whom Traver had previously called), Rachel, Michelle, Melinda, Claude Trudeau, and Arthur Lake. Traver almost jumped when he saw Moynihan's list.

"Are you calling Lake as a witness?" he asked. "Possibly," Moynihan answered. "I'm listing his name so that if I do call him you can't say I didn't list him."

The judge asked Traver, "Do you want to depose any of these witnesses?"

"No, that can drag this case out forever. I want to get I over as soon as possible."

"What about you?" The judge looked at Moynihan.

"I have the testimony of his witnesses from the first trial," Moynihan replied.

The judge then observed: "We may have a problem with the jury. Everybody has been reading about this case all over the country. We won't find anybody who does not know the facts of this case."

Traver was quick with an answer. "In my office we have given that considerable thought. So far as we are concerned, we don't care how much prospective jurors know. Moynihan may feel differently. To help matters, we will give him as many challenges as he wants to be sure he has a good jury. We don't want any problem on that score. I'm sure Tim won't be unreasonable in his objection."

I wondered whether Traver was very sure about his case or whether he was anxious to get it over with one way or the other. For this was a generous offer which the court might well overrule. The court said nothing. But Traver's remark had become part of the record of the pre-trial.

At the trial I was surprised at how short Traver's opening statement was. He simply set forth the facts about the nursing station, its location being next to Hannah's room and the location of the closet holding the vial of morphine. He described the location of the locker in which the nurses put their coats, even the kitchenette across the hall. Then he described briefly how the defendant had been at this location every day for weeks and told how the defendant wanted his wife dead and so used his knowledge of the station and procedures to obtain the vial of morphine, inject its contents in the tube carrying morphine to his wife and staying with her until she was dead before leaving.

Then he added, "You are going to hear a lot about love here, about how much the defendant loved his wife. But he also loved his business partner, a very beautiful and much younger woman. As you listen to their story about love, you will understand what the defense claims, the defendant loved both women, one was young and healthy, the other near death, in great pain, and wanting to die. The defendant was kind to both of his loves—killed the older one, took the younger one. Sound, kind, compassionate—that is no defense. Killing a person out of love is nonetheless murder. Love and compassion are not a defense."

Moynihan was also brief. In essence he said: "We don't claim love and passion excuse murder. We claim that with such love there can be no premeditated murder. You will not hear one word about jealousy or anger, or hate or indifference. You will hear only of love, devotion, and dedication. There is nothing in this case which shows one iota of intent or reason to kill. The so-called intent to kill exists solely in the mind of the prosecutor."

Arthur sat at his counsel's table. Martha, Michelle, Melinda, Claude and Rachel sat in the first row of seats directly behind counsel's table.

For Moynihan and for me—I was also at Defense counsel's table—the testimony of Traver's witnesses was "old hat." It was boring. Nothing new. I thought that his witnesses were a little more emphatic in their description of the conduct of Lake and Martha toward each other. Perhaps that was a very subjective evaluation on my part. I looked at the jury as the stories were told by the respective secretaries of the two about their embracing each other and how Martha had threatened to leave because she could not go on loving Arthur while Hannah was still alive. Of course the secretaries were not offering any more than they had at the first trial. It just seemed much more damning this time. I was unable to reach my conclusion as to the effect of this process on the jurors.

We were in the fifth day of the trial and Traver announced that his final witness was Dr. Morgan Archer.

"I am sorry, your honor," Traver said to the court as he rose from his chair. "I ask the court for a few minutes recess. Doctor Archer has not arrived, but he is due and I expect him any moment."

This was indeed unusual. Moynihan and I were stunned. But the court was not stunned. "Has the doctor been subpoenaed?"

"I'm sorry, your honor, I fully expect him to appear without a subpoena. He agreed to be here at this very moment."

"Do you know why he was delayed and how are we to know he will arrive here today?" The court was plainly irritated.

"Oh, I'm sure he will be here. He is not the type of person who would simply fail to show up."

At that moment Dr. Archer came into the courtroom. He went to Traver and whispered in his ear. A look of astonishment came over Traver. The whispering went on for a minute. The judge was about to pound his gavel when Traver said: "Your honor, I would like to have a few minutes recess. Doctor Archer wants to talk to me before he takes the stand."

Judge Carter now became testy. "Don't you usually talk to your witnesses before you ask them to attend a trial? This man was a witness at the first trial. I see no reason to delay this trial. There is no reason why the witness should not take the stand now."

"Your honor, I would like to recess to your chambers with counsel for the defense. I've been told something very new to this case and very important."

Moynihan nudged me. "I don't like this." Then he jumped to his feet. "Your honor, I don't think it behooves any of us to go off the record at this point. The whole world is waiting to see what happens here. Whatever it is it should be in open court so there can be no claim by the media that something new was first discussed and arranged for public disclosure in a closed meeting. This case has been tried continuously in the public media. I object to doing anything behind closed doors. Let's have it all right here and now in open court."

The court looked at Moynihan. "Do I understand that you object to a meeting between counsel and this court in the court's chambers?"

"I certainly do," Moynihan spoke firmly.

The court turned to Traver. "I think you can appreciate that I can't force Mr. Moynihan to have an 'off the record' session if he objects."

Now Traver became irritated. "Both the court and Mr. Moynihan know me well enough that I ask what I ask because it will facilitate matters. But if this must be handled in open court, so be it."

The judge rapped his gavel. "Present your witness, Mr. Traver."

Doctor Archer stepped up before the clerk. He carried a briefcase. He was duly sworn and sat in the witness chair.

Traver asked: "Did I not ask you to be in this court at three P.M. today?"

"You did."

"Are you here pursuant to my request?"

"I am."

"You have a briefcase with you. Do you have something in it which pertains to this trial?"

"I do."

"Will you please open your briefcase, take out what you have and present it to me?"

The witness opened the briefcase, took out a brown paper bag with something in it and handed it to Mr. Traver.

"Doctor, have I ever seen this object before?"

"No, sir."

"When did you obtain it?"

"This afternoon."

"How did you come by it?"

"It was brought to me by a chemist who works in the hospital laboratory."

Traver opened the brown bag and pulled out a glass vial. Arthur Lake exclaimed in hushed tones, "My God!"

"Doctor, will you tell the court and the jury what this is?"

"This is the vial of morphine which was locked in the closet at station number five on the day this all took place."

Moynihan jumped to his feet. Before he could say anything, Judge Carter said: "Mr. Moynihan, you chose to proceed in this manner." Moynihan sat down.

"How do you know this particular glass tube or vial is from the station involved in this case?"

"It has the station number on it."

"How did this exhibit get from the station to you?"

"This object was thrown in the trash bin at station number five. It went from there to the trash room. There it was recovered by Mr. Amory Thorton, a long-time employee of the hospital. He was under instructions to take to the pharmacy any container which held any drugs or medicines. We require this as a precautionary measure. Other hospitals have experienced drugs being smuggled out of the hospital through the trash. Mr. Thorton took this out of the trash at five o'clock on May eighth, the day of this incident. He could not get to the pharmacy because it was closed. He was scheduled to go see his grandson play on the high school baseball team and was already late so he put the vial on the cover of the top level of the shelf we keep in the trash room, intending, we surmise, to take it to the pharmacy in the morning. Mr. Thorton had a heart attack at the game and was dead when he was brought back to the hospital. The vial was discovered yesterday as the shelf was being cleaned to be repainted. The lab forwarded it to me and I have it here."

"Is there anything in this vial?"

"There is morphine in it."

"How much morphine?"

"The lab reported fifteen milligrams."

"How much can the vial hold?"

"Twenty milligrams."

"So only five milligrams were removed, or evaporated, is that right?"

"Yes."

"How long was the vial on the shelf?"

"We think from May eighth until yesterday, January tenth."

"Did anybody determine how much morphine was missing?"

"Obviously it was five milligrams."

"Doctor, if one were to receive five milligrams of morphine on top of ten milligrams would that be lethal?"

"No."

The court broke out into loud sounds. There were "Oh"s' and "Ah"s and words. People moved. Newspapermen got up and left the courtroom. Moynihan reached for Lake and embraced him. Martha, Melinda, Claude, and Rachel dashed to Arthur at the counsel's table.

The court rapped his gavel. "Order. Order," he cried. The noise subsided.

Traver now spoke. "I was trying to tell you, Judge, that this case is dismissed."

The court turned to Moynihan. "Any comments, Mr. Moynihan?"

"Yes, your honor," Moynihan responded. "Obviously we are happy with the prosecution's dismissal of the matter. I hope the court will understand if I ask to expand on this record. It is imperative that my client tell the rest of the story. We are on trial in the court of public opinion and that court will not be happy with the record as it stands. I want to call Mr. Lake to the stand. I also would like to retain the jury until my client's testimony is heard."

Arthur Lake was sworn and took the witness stand. Moynihan questioned him:

"Mr. Lake, on or about May eighth, 1984, did you at Heritage Hospital inject your wife, Hannah, with morphine?"

"I did."

"Where did you get the morphine and how did you put it into your wife?"

"Just as has been described by the witness for the prosecution."

Moynihan asked that the vial be placed into evidence. It was. Then he asked, "Is this the vial from which you took the morphine?"

"It is."

"I gather you did not empty twenty milligrams of morphine into your wife?"

"I did not."

"How much did you use and how did you measure the amount?"

"The vial is marked showing the number of milligrams which are contained. I tried to use three milligrams."

"But the vial shows five milligrams to be gone."

"I can't explain that. I can only guess that either I was not accurate in measuring or some of the contents have evaporated."

"Why did you limit the dosage to three or five milligrams?"

"Well, I certainly would not use the entire twenty milligrams. I had tried to research the use of morphine as a pain-killer. I went to the library and learned something. Then I went to my pharmacist and he told me that fifteen milligrams would be safe. I thought I was adding no more than three milligrams. Ten milligrams were not doing any good."

"Didn't you realize that you should not do what you did?"

"Sir, it was not a question of what I should or should not do legally or medically. It was a matter of stopping the pain. I could not bear to watch my wife suffer as she was suffering. The last thing I wanted to do was to kill her. I didn't understand why anybody would think I would want to kill someone I loved so dearly. That is insane."

"What did you do with the vial after you put some of the contents into your wife?"

"I put a plug on it so that the contents would be preserved. I had intended to show it to Doctor Archer to prove to him that an additional three milligrams helped relieve the pain without killing my wife. But one of the nurses was at the door. I panicked and threw it into the trash."

"Witness, do you love Martha Smith?"

"Yes."

"Did you love your wife?"

"Yes."

There was a pause. Then Lake continued. "Counsel, as you can guess I have had a lot of time to think about this. Apparently everybody forgets that you can come to love people with whom you work. There are many situations in which a man loves his wife and has at his workplace a secretary who may have been with him five, ten, fifteen, twenty years. She has looked after him, has studied him, learned his strengths and his weaknesses, his desires and his phobias. She thinks he is kind, honest, and considerate. And he is grateful to her. Let me tell you something. There are many, many cases in which a man falls in love with a woman with whom he spends most of each day and she treats him like a dear one."

I was astonished. I didn't realize Arthur Lake could be so eloquent—or that he would even venture such a speech. Moynihan hesitated. He wanted the jury, the judge, the press, everybody, to grasp fully what Lake had said. After the pause, Moynihan announced, "I have no further questions."

Traver declared he had no questions for the witness. The court leaned forward. "Am I to understand, Mr. Traver, that you wish to drop this case and the defendant to go free?"

"I am," Traver announced.

Moynihan was on his feet again. "I'm sorry, your honor, I cannot accept that."

Judge Carter seemed shocked. Before he could say anything Moynihan declared, "We will not accept a simple withdrawal of these proceedings. My client must be acquitted. For the prosecution to say it no longer wishes to press the matter still leaves Mr. Lake under an aura of suspicion and doubt. He is neither guilty or innocent.

"I would not make such a point of what might appear to the court to be picayune. I call to the court's attention that the defendant and Martha Smith have been tried in two courts—this court and the court of public opinion. When this retrial was ordered some magazine proclaimed that this court was wrong, and the public right. Today we have proof positive the defendant has committed no crime. My client could not have testified as he did today because he would have to admit he actually did administer morphine to his wife. Without the exhibit (he pointed to the vial of morphine) and with the admitted love of the defendant and Ms. Smith it was unlikely he would have been believed—and certainly not by the court of public opinion.

"Your honor, I move that this court direct that this jury return a verdict of 'not guilty.' "

Traver did not wait for the court to speak. He said simply, "No objection."

So, the court said to the jury: "Under the circumstances, I hereby direct that a verdict of 'not guilty' be entered. And you, the jurors, are excused and the accused released and his bond cancelled."

Near chaos followed. Newsmen dashed for the exists, cameramen poised outside the court soon rushed in. Michelle, Melinda, Rachel, and Martin rushed to Arthur Lake and engulfed him. Michelle reached out and pulled Moynihan and myself into the huddle.

Finally, Martha and Arthur walked away together. As they did so, Rachel came to me. "I remember," she said, "where at one of our picnics I heard Hannah say to Martha 'take care of Arthur. He is fragile. He loves deeply.' "

27

But what happened to Jimmy Smith? He had followed the case closely. After all, the bad talk before the new trial included him. He was suffering just as the others were. It was only a few days before the trial when he received a letter:

> Dear Jimmy,
>
> It has been a long time. And now you are suffering. Once before you came to me. Can I help you now?"
>
> *Jane Fairbanks*

A postscript listed her address and telephone number.

Jimmy put down the letter and called immediately. He almost shouted: "Jane, may I come over right away?"

There was a loud laugh at the other end of the line. "That's pretty much what you said to me the first time. I'm here. I'm waiting."

Jimmy immediately got into his car and drove to the area where Jane lived. He sensed he was being followed. So, he did not go to Jane's apartment building. He parked his car in a municipal parking lot and walked several blocks to an apartment house a block away from Jane's. He was amazed that two men followed him on foot out of the parking lot. They followed him to the apartment house Jimmy had chosen, though at some distance because he was not to know they were following him. He walked up to the door of the apartment house, opened it, and walked in. He entered a short hallway and there was nobody there. He then looked out through a small glass opening in the door and saw one of the men write down the address. Then the two men walked away. It was nearly ten o'clock in the evening. Used to being followed, Jimmy had hoped the late hour would discourage such antics.

Having gotten the address of the place where the great loverboy's current girl lived, the men left. Jimmy waited a few minutes and then walked to Jane Fairbank's apartment house.

She came to the door.

"What took you so long?" she asked.

"A couple of snoopers for some tabloid followed me and I had to lead them astray. Happens to me all the time."

They entered a tastily but modestly furnished apartment. He got a good look at the woman he had not seen for many years. Yes, she was older. But just as beautiful! He wanted to ask, Why did you run out on me? He didn't ask it. He also wanted to take her in his arms. He didn't. She took over.

"Once you came to me when you had problems. This time I knew you had problems and I came to you. Can I help you?"

He pulled her toward him, throwing his arms around her, saying nothing. Just holding her tight. "I only know that this is what I want to do, just hold you tight."

She had prepared some coffee, some drinks, and some biscuits. They sat at the dining table.

"I'm sorry this horrible case goes on and on," she began. "You don't deserve this notoriety. You've done nothing to make a part of this news."

"I have been a fool," Jimmy said, looking away from Jane. "I should have gone to Martha after our divorce. I was so wrapped up in myself, in getting ahead, that I forgot all about her. I'm afraid I never did love Martha. But I know she loved me; she is the only woman who has loved me all these years?"

"I loved you," Jane responded.

"Then, why did you leave?"

"Because you belonged to Martha. Maybe you didn't know that but I did."

"What are you saying?" Jimmy was puzzled.

"I'm saying that Martha was your wife, your mother, your father, your agent, your guardian. I left because I could never be all those things to you and I didn't think you could do on your own what she was doing for you. I'm no promoter, I have no scheme. All I want is somebody to love and who will love me. It's very simple for me. It was never simple for you. Yours was a very complex game involving a lot of people. All I ever wanted was just the two of us. I knew I could not have that."

"You know, Jane, that is all I want now. I'm tired of the flimflam, the make-believe, the hypocrisy. I'm ready for a simple love affair."

"Are you sure?" she asked.

"Try me," he replied.

"Okay, let's just get acquainted."

"We must do that in the sly," Jimmy cautioned. "If you are seen with me you will be smeared with me. I don't want that to happen."

"Okay, let's use this as our hideout, just as we once used Bonnie's and my room."

They talked and reminisced until the wee hours of the morning. They enjoyed each other and each was happy that sex was not the motivating force.

Jimmy and Jane continued this undercover affair for several weeks. They saw the trial end. The stories about Jimmy and Martha and Jimmy and Michelle soon evaporated.

Then one day Jane said to Jimmy: "I know how we can have a good time and not have to hide. Let's get married. Then nobody will give a damn what we do."

So, they found a district judge in a small town in California, were quietly married and issued a brief statement to the press. Life became much easier. Jimmy had been carefully guided financially by his agent, Walter Harman. He had some independent income and could work as he wished. The flashy public image was no longer necessary. Jane Fairbanks retired from her work, with a pension and became a busy housewife. She managed to follow the careers of Michelle and Melinda and reported to Jimmy.

When Martha and Arthur were married, she and Jimmy sent a gift with a note of congratulations, all engineered by Jane. Alas, she was now Jimmy's new manager!

The only unpleasant note to the story also occurred on my wedding day. Leaving the church, I discovered a ticket affixed to my windshield. I didn't fight it. A scorned woman should always be allowed to have the last word.

Epilogue

The letters to the editor did not stop with the end of People v. Lake. Two letters must be reported.

Letter one:

Dear Editor:

What happened to Arthur Lake and Martha Smith happened to me. I am retired, a happy housewife and grandmother. For thirty years I was the personal secretary to a man I respected and admired. He was a decent human being, honest, hardworking, kind, considerate, and thoughtful of others, including me. In good and bad times he was always the same. And there were many bad times. I suffered with him in bad times. I cared too much for him not to hurt when he hurt.

There came a time when business became very bad and my boss was abused by many people who knew nothing about our problems. More and more, day by day, he became more despondent. I couldn't stand it any longer. One day, when people had been particularly savage with him both in person and by telephone, at five o'clock I went into his office, closed the door behind me, saw him slumped over his desk. I went around his desk and stood beside him. I put both hands on his back and I said, very simply, "We must not let these people beat you. You are the best. I know. You will make it." He rose from his chair, took me in his arms, kissed me and whispered in my ear, "I love you." And I held on to him tightly and said, "And I love you."

I then tore myself from his grasp and without another word dashed out of the office, confused and terrified, fearful of what I had done. I drove home much too fast, ran into the house, greeted my husband and two teenagers, dashed into the kitchen and finished the evening meal which my daughter had started.

Fortunately my son and daughter began explaining their plans of the evening and my husband announced he had a golf match. Little more was said. The children cleaned the dishes. My husband took off. Soon I was alone.

And then it happened! I loved my husband and my children! And I could not be ashamed of what had happened to me at the office. In fact I was happy about it. I concluded I had done nothing wrong. I would have hated myself had I not done what I did. I smiled. Yes, I loved my husband and my children and I loved my boss as well! And I was happy that he loved me.

My boss and I found ourselves in each other's arms many times in the years that followed. We had an on-going love affair. Now we are both retired. He is a grandfather as I am a grandmother. We exchange Christmas cards and we see each other at the company Christmas party.

The greatest part of our relationship has been that we always honored our vows with our respective spouses. That's what permitted our "affair" to last for thirty years. Had we broken those vows there would have been hell instead of heaven.

I am the luckiest woman in the world.

Signed,
Another Martha Smith

Letter two:

Dear Editor,

I write about the Lake case on behalf of myself and thousands of women in circumstances such as mine. I'm divorced and with two children, as was Martha and as are many other women. I helped put my husband through college and law school. I raised two children and worked forty hours a week while he got his profession. When he was well established he divorced me and married a younger woman. I have continued to raise our children. His support money helps but my children have only one parent. Martha Smith stole another woman's husband in order to save herself.

Arthur Lake, in turn, took up with a younger woman, while still married to a crippled wife. They are both guilty of the betrayal of a helpless woman.

There are thousands of us betrayed women.

Signed,
A Victim